PRAISE FOR AK TURNER

". . . a rollicking, outrageous, hilarious adventure. Buckle up!"

—Michelle Newman, *You're My Favorite Today*

"Adventurous, funny, and inspirational, this book will convince you that traveling with kids isn't impossible. It's irresistible."

—Karen Alpert, *New York Times* bestselling author of *I Heart My Little A-Holes* and *I Want My Epidural Back*

"Everyone dreams of escaping the 9-to-5, but few have the guts to actually do it. AK dares to live her life on purpose and has realized early in life that true riches aren't reflected in accumulated possessions but are the vast and unique experiences we collect. If you're ready to dive into the digital nomad lifestyle, you must read this book. AK proves anyone can do it—even a family!"

—Christy Hovey, *The 9-to-5 Escape Artist: A Startup Guide for Aspiring Lifestyle Entrepreneurs and Digital Nomads*

Vagabonding
with kids
AUSTRALIA

Vagabonding
with kids
AUSTRALIA

AK TURNER

BROWN BOOKS
PUBLISHING GROUP

© 2017 AK Turner

Vagabonding with Kids: Australia

Brown Books Publishing Group
16250 Knoll Trail Drive, Suite 205
Dallas, Texas 75248
www.BrownBooks.com
(972) 381-0009

A New Era in Publishing®

ISBN 978-1-61254-919-4
LCCN 2016949847

Printed in the United States
10 9 8 7 6 5 4 3 2 1

Design by Sarah Tregay, DesignWorks Creative, Inc.
Cover photos by Amaura Mitchell and iStock
Author photo by Mike Turner

For more information or to contact the author, please go to
VagabondingWithKids.com or AKTurner.com.

For Mike

Because I am still, after nearly two decades,
wildly in love with you.

There are a lot of Mikes out there, though. And variations on Mike,
like Michael, Mica, Michelle, Michel, Mikhail, Misha, Miguel,
you get the idea. So if your name is one of those or something similar,
and you are not *my husband but want to pretend*
this book is dedicated to you, go for it.

QUEENSLAND

Buderim
Beerwah
Brisbane

Byron Bay

NEW
SOUTH
WALES

Port Macquarie

Fingal Bay

Sydney

Huskisson

Canberra
Murramarang

VICTORIA

Eden

Nowa Nowa

Melbourne   Lakes Entrance

BASS STRAIT

Devonport

TASMANIA

Hobart   Triabunna
White Beach   Rheban

TASMAN
SEA

N

CONTENTS

Welcome to Quarantine 1
Australian Disco 17
Don't Fear the Butcher 31
The Crocoseum 45
Humping the Dingo 63
A Formal Apology 75
Byron Bay 89
The Sex Lives of Koalas 103
Clean Is the New Black 113
Dry Is the New Clean 127
Killers in Eden 139
Take My Keys 151
The Spirit of Tasmania 159
Can I Get a Witness? 169
Port Arthur 181
Have a Solitary Christmas 191
Children and Other Devils 199
Adventures in Public Toilets 207
Love on the Beach 215
Burn Out 225
Taste of Tasmania 235
MONA 243
Dead on the Water 253
Melbourne Again 261
Idahome 271

Welcome to Quarantine

A 39-year-old Czech man was selected for a full baggage examination after he arrived on a flight from Dubai. During the examination, ACBPS officers conducted a frisk search of the man and allegedly found 16 small eggs concealed in his groin area.

—Australian Customs and Border Protection Service

Yellow tape designated the quarantine area, a narrow lane in the middle of the floor in which I attempted to keep my family corralled. I'd been quarantined, and they were bringing the drug dog my way. I told myself that the sweat mustache blooming on my upper lip, which has always been one of my more attractive features, had everything to do with the Australian heat permeating the building and worming its way into the Customs and Border Protection area, and nothing to do with the fact that I was being forcibly detained in the Customs and Border Protection area. There was no reason for worry. Illegal wildlife, weapons, and drugs occupied no part of my consciousness, much less my baggage, groin, or body cavity. Still, I continued to sweat, and the dog approached.

Twenty-four hours earlier, I stood in an airport in Idaho and thought, *I want to be married to the man doing lunges in the airport.* And luckily, I was. I watched as Mike instructed five-year-old Ivy on the proper posture of the perfect lunge. The image, endearing to me, could only have startled a stranger: there was my husband, a grown man lunging in a public area not typically suited for exercise, mirrored by a pony-tailed child clad in leggings, a rainbow tutu, and a shirt with a giant unicorn on the front.

"Like this, Daddy?"

"Yep," he answered. "Feel the burn."

I didn't join in on the lunging but later led a rousing game of Simon Says before Mike and I had the girls run ten laps around a large bank of seats, warning them to give other travelers a wide berth as they did so. Looking up to find an unknown child charging you in a maelstrom of pink and unicorns can be alarming, and I didn't want to be held responsible for the early death by heart attack of an unsuspecting business traveler.

Simon said all he had to say, and we couldn't force them to run any more laps, unless we wanted cruelty added to our list of parenting skills. Boredom commenced. The fact that we were dealing with the B word a mere hour into a twenty-four-hour trip was troublesome but undeniable. I knew it had taken hold when Emilia ratted out her little sister. "Mom, Ivy's licking the wall again."

"Ivy, please stop licking things." This is a command I speak more often than I care to admit. "Hey, I have a great idea!"

"What is it?" Emilia asked, her eyes wide with anticipation.

"Let's go to the *bathroom!*"

"Yeah!" They cheered and jumped with joy. This is contrary to the reaction I get when asking them to use the bathroom before leaving home. Public restrooms, however, are always a treat. Porta-Potties are especially revered, leading me to wonder if they share a faulty sense of smell.

Ivy and I took the handicapped stall while Emilia, eager to show her independence and maturity at the age of seven, went solo in the stall next to us. As soon as she was settled into what was apparently a much-needed urination, Ivy reached over and stuck her hand in the sanitary napkin depository. "What's this, Mama?"

"Don't touch that!" She withdrew her hand, and the metal lid closed with a creak. I heard an identical creak from the stall next to us as Emilia apparently withdrew *her* hand from her sanitary napkin depository, as well. I didn't bother explaining the receptacle's purpose. We'd been through the conversation many times before, and it hadn't done any good, because that odd little box on the wall just beckons. It's so intriguing. To them, it's one of the many perks found in a public restroom. This would not be the last time their hands acted on curiosity in an airport facility. Luckily, my children are as enamored with the sinks and soaps of public bathrooms as they are with the hidden treasures of the toilet stalls.

I waited until we exited the restroom to take a deep breath, visualizing myself inhaling excitement and exhaling fear. This is the type of action that I do often, but that if anyone *told* me to do, would immediately cause me to roll my eyes. I employ a variety of meditative tools, to which I would never admit, when we embark on months-long journeys to other countries. These quell the panic of the other me, who is a creature of habit and most comfortable when following a schedule so monotonous and predictable that it would make normal people opt instead to chew off their own feet.

When people ask why we travel for months at a time, the logical answer always seems to be *because we can*. In that regard, I have a lot in common with mountain climbers, who profess to climb mountains because the mountains are there. Actually that's a ridiculous lie, and there's no truth in the Everest analogy, because I'd keel over halfway to base camp. Either that or I'd bitch about the cold so much that one of my companion climbers would give me a well-timed nudge over a cliff, which I'd surely deserve. Nonetheless, we travel because the world is there, and we'd rather live in a place for months at a time than vacation there for a week. We're drawn to the challenge and intrigued by the logistical puzzle of living and working in another country. And anyone lucky enough to have the blessing-curse hybrid of self-employment might as well take advantage of the perk of mobility.

One hour and half a bottle of hand sanitizer later, we were on the flight to LAX when I realized that Ivy was a quarter of the way through one of the workbooks I'd purchased for her. One of the few materials that was supposed to last us months, and we weren't yet out of the country. *Well, obviously my child is gifted,* I reasoned, but I wanted to make it last, so we put the workbook away and replaced it with BrainQuest cards. These are flashcards, of sorts. They have pictures and require reasoning and deduction to get the correct answer. Some are more difficult than others. She whizzed through half the deck, again confirming my suspicions of her innate intelligence.

On a previous trip abroad, we'd enrolled both girls in a Montessori school, but the amount of moving around we'd undertake within Australia prohibited the possibility of them regularly attending a school. In planning the trip, Mike used the H word tentatively at first. As we discussed it, I often found that I couldn't say it without stuttering, so that it always came out as huh-homeschooling, as if I required a syllable of exhale before I could bring myself to utter the word in its entirety. I'd come to accept that I would (huh) homeschool the children, using a mix of materials, including those given to us by their teachers, online programs, workbooks, and a few supplemental fun activities, like the BrainQuest cards. I flipped the next card and read the question. "What part of your body should you wash before you eat a meal?"

"Your body?"

"No, Ivy. What *part* of your body?"

"Your teeth?"

"Ivy, what do we wash before we eat a meal?"

"Your head?"

The entire plane was learning that we were a filthy, disgusting family. Not only did my girls explore the sanitary napkin bin but they also didn't know what to wash before eating.

"Ivy," I took on a stern tone, as if that would somehow get her to say the correct answer. "What part of your body do you wash before you eat?"

"Your arms?" She said this loudly. Her increased volume was an answer to the increase in the severity of my tone. Either that or she wanted to make sure the entire plane heard.

"What do we do after we go potty?" I whispered. I thought maybe I could save face by getting her to say the correct answer, even if I had to cheat a little bit and alter the question.

"Wipe our private parts?" she boomed.

"Wash your *hands*, Ivy. You should always wash your hands before you eat a meal."

"Oh." She looked confused, as if this was the first time she'd ever heard such a ridiculous idea.

"I'll tell you what, Ivy. Let's put the BrainQuest cards away for a while. Do you want to play Would You Rather?"

"Okay," she answered. "I'll go first. Would you rather marry Daddy or have cake?"

"Ooh, that's a tough one." I *was* hungry. But again, my husband was the man not afraid to do lunges in the middle of an airport. And he was within earshot. "I'd rather marry Daddy."

We continued on with Would You Rather, with each of Ivy's questions to me involving some sort of confection, forcing me to choose between different forms of sugar. She posed the scenarios with desperation in her voice, as if nothing could be more heart wrenching than deciding on cake versus cupcake. Pitting cookie against brownie might as well have been *Sophie's Choice*.

The conversation struck me as sweet in more ways than one. When I flew as a child, the only topic I can remember talking about with my mother was death. We would weigh the odds of our plane crashing and joke about the improbability of a successful water landing, because let's be honest, if you crash in the ocean, you're not really going to slide down the ramp and board a little raft until safety arrives. Our morbid subject material wasn't relegated only to air travel. To this day, even with our feet firmly planted on the ground, conversations with my mother often turn to serial killers, unsolved murders, and other violent topics, which we are inexplicably compelled to share with each other. I can only hope for a similarly tender relationship with my own daughters as they mature.

Ivy and I weren't yet at that stage, though I often saw hints of it when she'd ask the questions, "Mom, when you die, will your hair still be there?" and "Mom, what would happen if a person touched fire to their eyeball?" For the flight, though, she was content to remain in the realm of sugar until we landed, presenting me with such difficult choices as, "Would you rather have a cake with pink frosting and purple sprinkles or purple frosting and pink sprinkles?" Oh, the dilemma.

At LAX, my least favorite airport on the planet but one in which I frequently find myself, Emilia remarked, "Lots of people here have brown skin." Statements like these reinforce my desire to travel with my children as much as possible. Life in Idaho can be blindingly white, though thankfully offset by Boise's emergence as a hub for refugees. As much as I love Idaho, I'm determined to show my daughters that the world is full of different people and cultures and thinking. And that all of those things are beautiful.

But perhaps LAX is not the best place to focus on such teaching moments. Because in the crush of harried travelers and high tensions, it's hard to look past the fact that it's just a big, loud, overcrowded, overpriced, and difficult-to-navigate airport full of ornery people and a pervasive lack of logic. And anyone who works at LAX should receive hazard pay for having to survive in such an environment. Or maybe one Xanax per shift.

We exited security, picked up our luggage, rechecked our luggage, and headed for security. The inefficiency of this process made me feel many things, not one of which was secure. The routine makes my heart race. I'm not afraid of the body scan or having every square inch of my luggage searched. It's a panic that I will inexplicably blurt out the word *bomb*, simply because I'm not supposed to. There's also the fear that in the rush of passengers removing belts and shoes and compulsively checking their boarding passes, I will lose something really important, like a child. Or a *computer*. Mike and I often look to our laptops as members of the family. There is a constant need to verify their proximity and health, because working overseas for months at a time only works if we are able to *work*. I passed through without being mistakenly identified as a terrorist, and in possession of one husband, two children, and my laptop.

By the time we took off for Brisbane, I wanted nothing more than to sleep. Ivy snuggled with heavy eyelids into her blankie, while Emilia fell asleep using the armrest as an awkward pillow. As she sank deeper into sleep, gravity took hold, and her lower jaw dropped down, while her top teeth remained caught, so that after a few minutes, her mouth was fully around the armrest, giving the impression that she was gnawing on something in her dreams. Her position amused but also disturbed me, as I viewed it even more unsanitary than sticking your hand in the sanitary napkin disposal box.

I looked across my daughters to Mike, who sat with his eyes serenely closed. My family was asleep. We had a fourteen-hour flight ahead of us. It was the perfect time for rest, and I needed sleep. But this was trumped by a shooting pain in my leg, which I was sure was a blood clot that would kill me. I was as sure of the blood clot as I had been when a swollen gland was lymphoma, which, of course, was really just a swollen gland, or when I had chronic jaw pain that was clear evidence of a tumor. And when I say chronic, I mean every so often for two and a half weeks. I mean, what constitutes chronic, really? But the bright side of the blood clot, if that was to be the cause of my demise, was that it would be much better than the other possibility of the plane going down. At least my family would be spared. Yes, good news indeed.

Qantas Airlines seemed like a safe bet. Australians are forced to innovate when it comes to travel, because when your country also occupies your continent, you have to get more adventurous than an extended road trip if you're going to venture internationally. And when you're surrounded by a number of oceans and seas, perhaps you dedicate a little extra thought to how best to cross them. Australians invented both the black box flight recorder and the inflatable escape slide, one of which implied a quest for truth in the face of tragedy, while the other seemed evidence of an inherently Australian optimism in the face of crashing into the ocean. I admired both perspectives.

While waiting for the blood clot to kill me, I settled in to make the best of my situation. I'd always thought Qantas would be luxurious. International flights, excluding short stints from the United States to Mexico, were supposed to carry with them a good deal of pampering, which is necessary to get otherwise rational humans through a fourteen-hour flight. But the Qantas flight had the same cramped discomfort that I associated with domestic flights. Sure, airlines had to cut costs, and airline travel no longer held the same exotic appeal that it once had, but still. To offer me alcohol only once during a fourteen-hour flight? What sort of cruelty was this? And why did the seats feel as tiny as those on a crappy little commuter plane? Had they been downsized too? A frightening but very real possibility struck me. What if the seats were the same size as they'd always been on international flights, but my ass was a few sizes bigger than the last time I'd traveled? The distance from my body to the back of the seat in front of me was also probably the same but seemed smaller now that my protruding belly required an additional allotment of this very precious real estate. And I wasn't even pregnant.

Other distances to contemplate were less distressing and far more interesting. Our plane would travel 11,575 kilometers from Los Angeles to Brisbane. I knew this because our flight data was plastered on the screen, which, because the occupant of the seat in front of me had reclined, was a mere two inches from my face. Along with 11,575 kilometers across the Pacific Ocean came the element of time travel. We left the United States on a Sunday night and after the fourteen-hour flight would arrive in Brisbane on Tuesday morning, leaving the Monday in the interim lost in time. It simply would not exist for us, though if you have to lose one day of the week, I guess Monday would be the one to go. We would regain this time, of course, on the way back, when we'd depart Australia on a Tuesday morning, and after twenty hours of flying on four different planes, and six hours of layovers in three different airports (one of which was sadly LAX), we'd arrive to find it only Tuesday afternoon.

Emilia stirred next to me, dislodged her jaw from the armrest, and sat up. I wanted to share with her the magnitude of these facts.

"Emilia, do you realize that we're traveling 11,575 kilometers?" I pointed to the data on the screen in front of me.

"Wow," she said, nearly punching me in the face as she stretched. "That's a lot. I think I need to write that down for part of my homework." I retrieved a homework folder with questions for her to answer on the plane. "How many miles are we traveling?" she asked.

"I'm not sure how many miles, but it's 11,575 kilometers. Isn't that amazing?"

"Yes, but how many *miles* is it?"

"It's thousands!" I was trying to maintain the sense of wonder but felt failure creeping in. I've never been good at converting things, from units of measurement to the convertible bra.

Emilia sighed. "That doesn't really help me, Mom."

The following day, I would look it up and give her the number 7,192. This would be the first of many disappointing instances of completing homework in which I employed Google and fed her the answer.

Emilia and Ivy passed the time in a rotation of eating, sleeping, and watching movies. The presence of individual televisions on international flights makes them oddly more bearable than shorter, domestic flights, and it's a wonder that I felt any discomfort, given that eating, sleeping, and watching movies are three of my favorite pastimes.

Hours later, as we began our descent into Brisbane, the flight attendant made an announcement that no food would be permitted through customs. Not even food from the airplane. My girls each had a purse. One was pink with a rainbow of sequins, the other pink with *My Little Pony*. Both were chock-full of various airplane snacks that I'd been hoarding away over the last twenty hours. I'm compelled to save every ration of pretzels and peanuts, because I feel it's my right after spending thousands of dollars on airfare. I want my rightful snacks, whether I consume them or not.

The plane landed safely, at which point I had to admit to myself that our Australian adventure was actually going to happen. The blood clot didn't make it to my brain or my heart or wherever it needed to go to kill me, and the biggest failures of the flight were my inability to convert kilometers to miles and the crew's failure to offer me more than one alcoholic beverage. Mechanical failure wasn't even in the running, despite the fact that I'd spent the previous six months vacillating between excitement and certainty that the plane would go down. Neither the black box flight recorder nor the inflatable escape slide would be needed.

"Mom, can I have the Kit Kat now?" Emilia asked.

"Not right now, sweetie." Two tiny Kit Kat bars were part of the hoarded stash of food, but I had to put my go face on and wrangle luggage and children. I wasn't equipped to deal with chocolate-covered children. "We'll have them later."

We disembarked and walked down a long corridor, dotted with signs on how food was not allowed through customs. These signs were placed over trash cans, encouraging travelers to dispose of any food items they might be carrying. But how could I throw away perfectly good food? That seemed unnatural. So I continued on. But then I hesitated. I am innately a rule follower.

"Mike, do you think I should ditch this stuff?" I motioned to one of the girls' purses, brimming with an assortment of wrapped goodies.

"Now can I have the Kit Kat?" Emilia asked.

"No," I answered.

"It's fine," Mike said offhandedly.

Right, it's fine. There's nothing to worry about. Stop being such a rule follower, I chided myself. We got in line for immigration, where a man approached me and asked to see my customs form. "Do you have any food?" he asked.

"Uh."

"Just tell me now."

"Just some stuff from the plane," I fessed and flashed him one of the cereal bars from the *My Little Pony* purse. He waved us on, and I relaxed.

"Mom, I have to pee," said Emilia.

"Well, you'll just have to wait."

It occurred to me then that while Mike had taken Ivy to the bathroom twice on the plane, because he's one of those phenomenal husbands who doesn't push every distasteful task onto his wife, Emilia hadn't used the bathroom once during the entire flight. Which was great, because no one actually enjoys using a bathroom on a plane, even my Porta-Potty-loving kids. But Emilia hadn't peed in about sixteen hours. Was that normal? Had I subconsciously dehydrated my own child to avoid taking her to the airplane bathroom?

"I can wait," she said, and I thought that she must have inherited her dad's bladder capabilities, as Mike urinates twice daily while I go about every forty-five minutes, not including involuntary urination, which happens whenever I sneeze. "But *now* can I have the Kit Kat?"

"No, Emilia." I really wanted her to shut up about the Kit Kat. I pictured myself doing time in an Australian prison for attempting to smuggle a Kit Kat into the country.

After immigration, we retrieved our substantial luggage and, with form in hand, entered a line to go through customs. And I should have known better. Because whenever you travel for more than ten days, you get the full search. We would be in Australia for months.

Before I knew it, there I was in the quarantine line. And the drug dog was heading my way. Staring at me as if to say, *I can smell those chocolate-covered wafers you're hiding. I know about the salted nuts.* My sweat mustache bloomed again in all its glory. I was going to end up in jail over a Kit Kat. And not even one that I would get to eat. And not even a full-sized candy bar. This thing was pathetically small, smaller even than Halloween candy. The dog inched closer and then moved past the *My Little Pony* purse without a moment's hesitation. My heart pounded. *I got away with it,* I thought. *I'm an international smuggler.* Sure, it's not like I had four pounds of hashish strapped to my body, but still. Then the dog sat down. Her handler took hold of the other purse; the rainbow of sequins apparently failed to portray innocence. The handler opened it and rifled through the cereal bars and pretzels, seeming not to care about them at all. I felt relief again. These minor snacks didn't matter. I had been worrying over nothing. Until her hand withdrew from the purse a shiny red apple. And she looked at me as if condemning Eve for her transgression. Mike looked at me with the same disdain, a look that said, "Do I even know you?"

That's when shit got serious. Every inch of luggage was searched. The apple was confiscated and placed in a plastic bag. We were handed over to the care of a new customs officer. I'd filled out the customs forms. I'd packed the bags. I claimed responsibility. And only for a second did I contemplate throwing one of my children under the bus. Because surely they wouldn't send a child to do time for the apple.

"You have violated Australian Quarantine Law. We could fine you. We could give you up to ten years in prison." He paused for effect.

I almost blurted, "But it's an apple!" but didn't want to suffer the spiel of the potential harm of my environmental violation.

"But none of that will happen today. Instead we're going to give you a warning." On a photocopied paper that detailed the penalties I could have faced, he wrote my name. Even my middle name, which made it seem extra serious.

When we made it through, I was furious with myself for not listening to my instincts and throwing away all of the snacks when I had the chance. I'd wanted to, but I also wanted to be the type of person who was relaxed and casual and moved about the world without constantly worrying about trivialities. And it's these two warring desires that screw me.

"See," I said to Mike. *"This* is why I'm a rule follower. I should have just ditched everything. But *you* told me not to worry about it." I burned with humiliation, fumed like a child caught cheating.

"Yeah," he said, "but I didn't know you had an *apple."*

"It's not like it was a poisoned apple!"

"You can't mess around with fruit. They take that *very* seriously."

As much as I wanted to be angry with Mike, I was angry with myself. I'd failed. And yet we were free to go, embarking on a monumental journey. We were officially Down Under. And a small part of me felt like an international ninja smuggler, because there was still that matter of the Kit Kat. And *that* fucker made it through.

* * *

Australian Disco

*Of the 828 bird species listed in Australia,
about half are found nowhere else.*

—Tourism Australia

Our first morning in Australia, we were wakened at 4:30 a.m. by a swelling cacophony. It began with chirps and delicate tweets. A laser-like birdcall chimed in, and I felt I'd fallen inside of a giant video game. The laser was the call of the eastern whipbird, not to be confused with the lyrebird, which makes an entirely different laser-like sound, also reminiscent of a video game but perhaps from a different weapon. The kookaburra joined in next, which I would have sworn was a monkey. By the time I was fully conscious, I had the odd image in my head of a troop of primates, geared in helmets and elbow pads, creeping in the jungle outside our bedroom window, engaged in an epic battle of laser tag. *The Planet of the Apes* image persisted, despite the fact that I was on the only continent that has rain forests but no monkeys. Against all logic, I peered out of the windows to search for them. Not only did I fail to see laser-wielding monkeys but I also didn't see any of the birds responsible for the noise. The view was of a thick jungle, in which one towering tree couldn't be distinguished from the next, a riot of green in vines, stalks, fronds, and ferns.

We had arrived the day earlier to a hilltop home on the edge of a rain forest on the Sunshine Coast. We exited a shuttle and hiked a steep driveway. The air was dense and humid, and we breathed heavily, dragging our luggage (minus one confiscated apple and two devoured Kit Kats) and children. Approaching the front door signified the merciful end to our twenty-four hours of travel from Idaho.

A long-limbed, sleek woman opened the door.

"Hello!" I smiled. "We made it."

"Yes." She smiled back before a poorly masked shade of fear swept her face. "Oh, you have little ones." Her body blocked the doorway, as if physically conveying that she had changed her mind, that we would not be allowed entry, that she was turning us away and we'd better run down her impossibly steep driveway, begin flailing our arms to hail our shuttle, and start the long journey back to Boise.

"Yes," I confirmed, looking down at my not-so-little little one. "This is Ivy." I wanted to add: *She is one of my two children, whose existence and ages were disclosed to you ten months ago when we began discussing this arrangement.* But I didn't.

"Well," she tried to recover her smile and resigned herself to the inevitable, "come in."

Our host was both an artist and art collector and possessed the type of grace that made the term *artist* too pedestrian for her. *Artiste* made more sense. Her home was ours for four weeks, in a complex system of home exchanges. She took us on a tour of the house, in which everything was either white or made of glass, save for bright red paintings, precarious sculptures, and a grand piano.

"Ooh, Mom, can I play the piano?" Emilia asked.

"No." I shot a look at her that said, *Please be silent and still until the Artiste leaves.* Emilia did not get the message.

"This," the homeowner said, gesturing to the piano, "is a family treasure." My daughters' eyes lit up at the mention of treasure. This would make them want to touch it more. "And I ask that you not set anything on it, aside from papers."

Mental note: *Don't touch the family jewels. Don't set anything on it, even paper. Convince kids there is no treasure hidden inside the piano.*

One of the bedrooms had two children's beds, but I still had the impression that the Artiste was not at ease among children and could only assume the bedroom existed for the occasional and likely brief visits of grandchildren.

The master bathroom was home to a giant soaker tub.

"Ooh, look at the bathtub!" Ivy squealed.

"Please don't use this tub," instructed the homeowner. "It uses too much water, and water here is so very scarce."

She spoke in earnest as someone who felt a deep connection to the land, someone who had felt the plague of drought and ached in her heart because of it. I promised that we would be conscientious of our use of water, and I meant it. We'd take quick showers, and our children would bathe in the smaller tub with minimal water. I'd subdue my passion for sterility to preserve this precious resource. I would *not* be a wasteful, inconsiderate tourist.

We followed her into the living room. "As you can see, everything here is just so dry." Her voice still had the pain of one who had long tried to farm drought-stricken land. And as she spoke, she gestured out to her magnificent view, which showed an endless expanse of the lushest, thickest, greenest rain forest I'd ever seen.

The tour continued outside where she introduced me to two-dozen potted plants tucked underneath her deck, which I was to water twice a week. Another mental note: *Conserve water at all costs. Except when it comes to potted plants hidden under the deck.*

Eventually there was nothing left to show us, so she handed over the keys and left, which I'm sure pained her. Home exchanges sound wonderful until you relinquish your dwelling, with all of its treasures and your accumulated possessions, to strangers. I didn't fault her for her obvious discomfort but felt relief when she finally departed. And then Ivy began fondling a statue of a bare-breasted woman, poking at the nipples and inserting her hand in the cleavage. I silently thanked her for waiting until the Artiste had gone. In the coming weeks, Ivy would create a ritual of fondling the statue, grasping a breast with each passing.

When we'd settled in and properly molested the artwork, Mike called one of his friends from college who, as fate would have it, lived in Australia with his wife and two children, not far from our accommodations in Queensland. Levi is a ship's pilot in Alaska, bringing foreign vessels into Yakutat, Ketchikan, Glacier Bay, and Sitka, among other harbors, a job that allows him to work only part of the year and live and play anywhere else in the world the rest of the time. We hadn't seen him in over a decade and were excited about the reunion. When he arrived that afternoon, we found that he hadn't changed much in the previous ten years, other than having acquired the roles of husband and father, at which he excelled. From Mike's college days, I remembered Levi as exceedingly kind and optimistic, the type of person for whom every expression is some version of a smile.

"So good to see you guys!" he gushed upon arrival. "Do you have a car? Do you want one of ours?" When a friend you haven't seen in years hands his car over to you, asking for nothing in return, you know he's a keeper.

Levi drove us to his home in Coolum where we visited with his family. Our daughters discussed their favorite *My Little Pony* pony while the adults chatted over a beer. "Should we walk down to the beach?" Levi suggested. "It's just a short walk, and there's a playground for the kids."

Short is relative. If you're talking about distances comparative to a marathon, then I would concede that two miles is short. But when you add a five-year-old who thinks that tutus and sparkly shoes are good hiking gear, two miles is torturous, for the parents more than the child.

Along the way, we stopped to observe a tree brimming with fruit bats, and I marveled every time great white cockatoos swept overhead. The vision of cockatoos flying free caused me to waver between a desire to return to vegetarianism as a show of solidarity with all living creatures, versus my competing desire to try a meat pie from a fast-food joint we'd passed called Beefy's.

When we reached the playground, the kids showed off their climbing skills while the adults gazed out at the ocean.

"So, just how likely are we to die here?" I asked. I was joking. Mostly.

Levi laughed and proceeded to educate me about Surf Life Saving Australia, a volunteer organization that serves as lifeguards, monitors shark activity, and wears adorable little beanies, all of which convinced me that my family might actually survive the trip.

"But *how* do they monitor shark activity?" I asked.

"They have shark nets set up."

"Nets?"

"Well, they're not actual nets, but they're called shark nets. There are baited buoys, and they monitor the bait."

"Wait, so they're *baiting* the sharks into the beach?" Maybe survival wasn't probable, after all.

"Don't worry, Amanda. They're monitored way offshore, they have helicopter patrols, and you're going to be just fine."

"Okay," I said, while silently wondering how I could keep my family from going in the water.

"Mom," Emilia interrupted. "Can we go in the water?"

"We will another time, Emilia. I promise. But not today, because we don't have our swimsuits."

"Okay, Mom," she said, at which point both Emilia and Ivy hiked up their skirts and went in anyway. I didn't protest, which was my way of acknowledging that passing on my disproportionate fear of water to my daughters would be less than responsible parenting.

Before we departed that day, Levi and his wife invited us to return in a week for Thanksgiving dinner.

"That would be great," I said. Thanksgiving is easily my favorite holiday, because it requires no decorations and presents while still allowing me to gorge on food and drink. And because we were in Australia through the fall and winter, I'd assumed I'd miss out on the gluttony of the season altogether. "What would you like me to make?" I asked.

"Amanda can make *anything*," Mike said. I blushed at my husband's confidence in me but also silently recognized that my culinary skills don't translate well in foreign kitchens with unfamiliar ingredients. It was decided that I'd contribute a casserole and a pumpkin pie, which were well within my capabilities.

With our plans of overindulgence in place, Levi's wife handed over the keys to her Subaru for us to borrow for the next week or so. Our kids climbed in the backseat while Mike and I clumsily approached the wrong sides of the vehicle before realizing our error, as well as the fact that this wasn't likely to inspire Levi's confidence in us. I walked back around to the left side of the vehicle and felt odd sitting with no steering wheel in front of me. Mike sat in the driver's seat and placed his left hand on the stick shift.

"You can do this," I said.

"I know I can do this. I'm not worried."

"Okay, good. Because you shouldn't be. And don't worry about the fact that they're standing there watching us and that you have to back out of this extremely long and narrow driveway."

"I love you," Mike said, "but I'm going to have to ask that you stop speaking."

We waved meekly at Levi and his wife and slowly made our getaway. I clenched my teeth in anticipation of the crunch of metal, which thankfully never came.

Driving required Mike to display his freakishly competent skills at navigating a car on the left side of the road, with the driver's seat on the right side of the car. And because the car was a stick shift, he shifted with his left hand, so that first gear was away from the body. Trying to comprehend all of this hurt my brain and made me constantly question the concepts of left and right. Mike managed with little problem, though for the first few days I heeded Levi's advice by repeating the steady reminder of "Keep left, keep left, keep left." I thought it was nice of Australia to accommodate foreigners with the Keep Left signs dotting the highway.

As we drove between beach towns on the Sunshine Coast, I scanned the landscape for wildlife, hoping for my sake as well as my children's that the first kangaroo we saw wouldn't be roadkill. I was sure that every tree was home to a koala that wanted to crawl down and cuddle with me. Though the wildlife didn't make itself known on that first afternoon, we did drive by magnificent flame trees and brilliant purple jacarandas, giving the landscape the appearance of a green, orange, and violet Pollock canvas.

With our borrowed car and finagled home, I felt pretty comfortable about settling in for our journey. As our first full day in Australia came to a close, Mike and I sat down with a glass of wine. Everything felt in place and as it should be.

"We made it," I said with a smile.

"I'm freaking out," said Mike.

"What? What are you talking about?" I'd had such a feeling of ease a moment before. For Mike to be freaking out, there had to be something I didn't know. Did he have a secret gambling addiction, and loan shark thugs were tracking us down? Had he been running a Ponzi scheme, and the feds were closing in? Was that why he'd been so amenable to leaving the country? Or was it another woman? Could I anticipate a *Fatal Attraction* psycho sneaking into our borrowed home? I would take that bitch *down!*

"We don't have any plan for what we're going to do after we leave this house," Mike said. "We don't know where we're going to live for the second half of the trip."

"Yes, but we just got here. This is day one."

"I know."

"For the past six months, every time I tried to plan the rest of the trip, you told me to relax."

"Because you were freaking out," he said.

"But I was only freaking out so that we'd have everything in place and could avoid *this*. I wanted to avoid a freak-out during the trip."

"Maybe we just have different ideas about when it's the appropriate time to freak out," he reasoned. "In any case, we're here, and I'm panicking because we don't have anything figured out."

"Stay calm," I commanded. "You're not having a regular freak-out."

"I'm not?"

"No. You're having the *traveler* freak-out."

"I am?"

"Yes. I know what you're feeling. It happened to me when we were in Mexico for three months. Remember?"

"Yeah." He nodded. "But you were questioning the meaning of life and stuff."

"The traveler freak-out comes in many different forms."

It's true, and a condition well known to part-time digital nomads like ourselves. Emotions run high, and panic sets in, bringing with it all manner of questions, including what the hell are we doing here, what is the meaning of life, how can we possibly afford this, and how *does* sand manage to get its way into the bed despite all of my efforts to the contrary.

To remedy the freak-out, we spent days making plans for the rest of the trip. This involved dozens of phone calls during which we learned that hotels and rental units were booked.

We are never as original as we suppose, and the idea of escaping winter by traveling to summer on the other side of the world was not solely ours. The lack of available accommodations intensified Mike's stress level. We'd relax every time we had another piece of the itinerary puzzle in place, then add more debt to our credit card to secure our reservations, which spawned an entirely new avenue for freak-outs.

In planning the rest of the trip, we knew we wanted to head south to Tasmania, and we also wanted to see more of Australia along the way, so we decided to book a small RV, travel down the coast for a few weeks, and then stay in a few places in Tasmania. In reality, we didn't so much *decide* where to stay in Tasmania as book anything that was available.

As we looked at places to camp along the coast of the mainland, we viewed websites for dozens of campgrounds with events for kids.

"Ooh, look at this place," Mike said. "They have an event called Kids' Disco and Karate!"

"Wow, that's ambitious." I tried to wrap my head around it. Did they incorporate karate moves into dance? Did you learn how to break a cinder block while doing the hustle? "Australian disco must be really awesome, being the home of ABBA."

"Tell me you didn't just say that," Mike scowled.

"ABBA? Not Australian?"

"Swedish."

"Oh, right. I was thinking of the Bee Gees."

My husband looked at me as if I'd punched him in the gut. "What?"

"British."

"Right. Okay, so maybe Australian disco isn't really a thing. I still don't understand Kids' Disco and Karate." I pictured a four-year-old in a tiny karate gi and headband, dancing to "I'm Your Boogie Man" under a disco ball. Whenever I fail to connect a phrase in my head, I remind myself to stop and consider the source. I looked at what Mike was reading.

"You mean Kids' Disco and *Karaoke*," I corrected.

"Oh." He looked disappointed. "Kids' Disco and Karate sounded so much cooler."

We finalized our camping itinerary (sadly without the inclusion of disco, karaoke, or karate) down the east coast of Australia, and I wondered how we'd make the transition going from the opulence of our borrowed home in Queensland to living in a souped-up van with two kids. The thought made me claustrophobic.

Once we had a plan in place for the rest of our travels, Mike calmed down, and we settled into enjoying our surroundings, searching out places and activities that were distinctly Australian, and ignoring the American culture that seemed to be everywhere. McDonald's is as pervasive as religion throughout the world, which makes me feel oddly ashamed, but beyond that, we saw T-shirts advertising UFC or branded with US locations like Brooklyn, Indianapolis, and California. Billboards pushed Coke in a rainbow of cans, and we encountered the usual suspects of Starbucks and 7-11 and Walmart. Perhaps the most depressing American encroachment was Sizzler. You just don't want to fly to the other side of the world and see a Sizzler. At least I don't. As a result, I would gravitate toward anything that gave the impression of being inherently Australian, which often incorporated an air of relaxed friendliness and an appreciation for the landscape itself.

After two days, my awe and appreciation of the rain forest outside of our bedroom window was tempered by my desire to shoot the birds. I recognized my human arrogance and the fact that the birds' presence was far more natural than my own, so instead I instituted the habit of waking at four in the morning to shut the windows, which we left open at night in the hope that cool air would work its way inside, before the cacophony reached its crescendo. At least the birds were outside. Inside, we'd dispatched a fair number of insects and one giant arachnid, which thankfully my girls did not see. They did, however, witness a few cockroach encounters.

I stood in the hallway one evening as they sat on the couch in the living room.

"It's time to get ready for bed, girls."

"What?!" Emilia said indignantly, as if I don't utter these same words at the same time, every evening of her life.

"Come on. Let's brush teeth and go potty."

Ivy sulked as if I'd asked her to learn Latin, but both girls trudged my way.

"Wait," I snapped. "Hold on just a second."

A light brown roach perched on the wall next to me, and I wanted to dispose of it while they were still at arm's length.

"What's wrong?" Emilia asked.

"Oh, nothing," I answered. "Hand me the newspaper on the coffee table, would you?"

She did so, then seeing the bug, took another step back.

"It's okay, just a little insect. I'll take care of it." I was trying to sound casual. I didn't want my daughters to gain an unnatural fear of bugs. But my casual tone infected my actions, and when I swatted at the roach, it was more lackadaisical than I'd intended. As soon as I failed to hit the bug, the roach demonstrated that it had wings. It flew directly from the wall to my bare calf and sprinted up my dress. I began a frantic, high-stepping hop, all the while trying to keep my face placid for the benefit of my kids, the combination of which somehow caused me to drool on my own breasts.

"Mom, are you okay?" Ivy asked.

"I'm fine," I said calmly, while stomping as hard as I could in an effort to dislodge the roach from my thigh. "I just didn't expect that sucker to fly." The bug hit the floor, and I crushed it with my flip-flop over and over again.

"Mom," Emilia said. "I think it's dead."

"Yes," I said, out of breath and flushed. "Nothing to worry about."

I'm not sure why having a roach on my body is so terrifying. It's not going to bite me or sting me, and if it defecates on me, the resultant matter will be microscopic, and I won't ever know about it. But there's the lurking fear that one day I will encounter a roach that intends to burrow into my body and begin colonizing there, so I was unable to react in any way other than hopping around in a move that I came to think of as the Australian disco.

* * *

Don't Fear the Butcher

Mulesing Sheep: In 1937, the CSIRO (Commonwealth Scientific and Industrial Research Organisation) recommended a technique developed by the South Australian grazier J.H.W. Mules to remove the skin around a sheep's anus where blowflies might lay their eggs. The technique is regarded as cruel by animal liberation groups in the US.

—David Dale, *Who We Are: A Miscellany of the New Australia*

"We were thinking of taking our kids swimming at a local pool this afternoon," Levi said over the phone. "Would you guys like to come?"

I was about to ask if we could bring beer when he added, "They have lanes set up too, so if you want to swim some laps while we're there, you can."

"Great," I lied and decided to withhold my alcohol inquiry.

The pool experience highlighted stark differences between our families. While Mike and I looked toward the snack stand, lamenting the fact that they didn't serve beer and trying to decide whether we'd order a meat pie, sausage roll, or both, Levi eyed the swimming lanes. His three-year-old daughter swam on par with our seven-year-old, and his one-year-old appeared braver in the water than five-year-old Ivy.

"I'll make a list of all the things to do around here," Levi promised as we bobbed in the water and pretended that it's somehow fun to be splashed in the face by our kids. "There's a great forest walk right by where you're staying in Buderim."

Huh, I thought. *Good to know I've been butchering the name of our town.* It's closer to BUDrim, while I'd been telling the world we'd be spending a month in booDERum.

"You'll definitely want to check out the beach at Mooloolaba," he continued.

Crap. How many times had I said MOO-LOO-lah-bah? Only to learn now that it was actually muh-LOO-la-bar. The R at the end is almost implied as opposed to pronounced, like many words ending in a vowel. Ivy would repeatedly ask Levi's daughter why she called Emilia *Emiliar.* The phantom R is ironic to Americans, as when there is an *actual* R at the end of a word, like river, Australians will drop it. Rivah.

"And Noosa, of course, is my favorite."

I decided that Noosa would be my favorite, as well, as there was no possible way for me to butcher the pronunciation. "There's a fantastic kayak trip you can take from Noosa."

"With kids?" Mike asked.

"Yeah," Levi answered. He motioned to his wife. "We each had one kid in front of us in the kayak, and it was no problem. But be prepared; it's quite a trek."

Mike and I looked at each other as if to say, *No way in hell.* If something was a trek for Levi, chances are it would kill us.

The next day, we took Levi's advice on which beaches and attractions to check out on the Sunshine Coast, barring any epic kayak trips and starting with Mooloolaba. I found the beach a shockingly beautiful introduction to the Coral Sea, which says something, considering that I'm not much of a beach person. I would later learn that nearly every beach we encountered in Australia was shockingly beautiful. Pristine sand bled into brilliant sapphire waters under a clear, expansive sky. As someone raised on the East Coast of the United States, in Chesapeake Bay territory, I'd come to expect large bodies of water to have a brownish hue.

Pristine and manicured, Mooloolaba was also fairly commercial. An esplanade paralleled the beach with restaurants and shops and psychics, which always seem plentiful in tourist beach areas. Maybe vacationers are more likely to patronize a psychic because there's less danger of being spotted by your neighbor as you enter. Or perhaps it's just the indulgent nature of vacation that lends itself to such things. As a teenager, my best friend and I patronized a psychic in Ocean City, Maryland, where we paid five dollars for such vague predictions as "You will fall in love, and he will have an M or a J in his name." As a hormonal sixteen-year-old, this was exactly what I wanted to hear, and I felt my five dollars was well spent. After all, my husband's name is Mike.

High-rise hotels and apartments backed the shopping boulevard. There were beachfront areas designated for campers and public toilet and shower facilities that were cleaned multiple times a day, for which I was thankful, given how often my children demanded to visit them.

"Would you ever want to live in a place like this?" Mike asked. I looked to the esplanade and saw, along with bottles of wine and elegant dresses for sale, mounting debt. As if reading my mind, Mike qualified his question. "You know, if money didn't matter."

"I don't know." I looked to the beach. "If you live at the beach, there's just so much . . . sand."

"Okay, but let's say you had a pool too. So every time we came back from the beach, we could dunk the kids in the pool before letting them inside."

While Mike doesn't share my intense and irrational aversion to sand, he knows that he must deal with it if he wants me to say yes to such hypotheticals as living in Mooloolaba. But the fact that the hypothetical required complete denial of financial realities combined with anti-sand tactics told me that chances are we will never live in Mooloolaba.

After our first afternoon at Mooloolaba, as we drove back to Buderim, Mike suggested we stop at the grocery store.

"I don't know if now's the best time," I said. "We're all sandy and in our bathing suits."

"There you go again with the sand."

"Well!"

We'd covered ourselves with other clothes, but I still didn't feel appropriate entering a grocery store.

"Amanda, we're in Australia."

Mike was right, and when we entered the grocery store, I noted the man and his son without shirts and shoes, and the many other shoppers who also appeared to have just come from the beach. This isn't lazy or unhygienic but a confirmation of America's ridiculously uptight inclinations. It also didn't hurt that the scant clothing of recent beachgoers was mostly attributed to surfers, both male and female. I knew that I would have felt differently about the relaxed manner of dress had the shoppers not all been in peak physical condition. I made a mental note to offer an extra smile as a show of solidarity to anyone I encountered who, like myself, was not in possession of surfer abs.

Even when surrounded by extremely fit specimens of the human body, it's tempting in a new place to eat out, go big, and pretend it's a vacation, but that's a mistake when doing extended travel. We needed cheap and easy foods to counter the fortune we'd spent on airfare and future accommodations. We sought cereal, bananas, carrots, hummus, granola bars, apples, and the makings of peanut butter and jelly sandwiches. When the cart was piled high, I pushed it toward one of two available lanes but then saw the familiar look of panic on Mike's face, the look he gets whenever he's faced with the prospect of having to wait in line. Both lanes were five customers deep, which is Mike's personal hell. You'd think that someone who travels often and extensively would handle this better, because what is an airport if not a succession of lines in which to stand?

He grabbed the cart and steered it toward the self-checkout lane, which, just as in the States, was not designed for people buying an entire cart full of food.

"Mike, what are you doing?"

"Just go with it."

He fell into a mode of rapid-fire bar code scanning, hurling items at me to bag, though we quickly ran out of room. Now the self-checkout lane was as backed up as the others.

"Mom, my feet hurt," Emilia whined.

"Mom," Ivy said, "I have sand in my—"

"Not now, girls," I said. "I know you're tired. Just please be patient for one more minute."

When all of our items were scanned, I swiped my credit card. The screen flashed and then instructed me to "present the card." Present it how? I turned to the attendant who'd been surveying us with a mix of awe, pity, and annoyance and displayed my card. Likely, I was meant to present it to her.

"No," she said. "You need to *present* the card."

I moved it closer to her, just a few inches from her face. Maybe she wanted me to display it so that she could really see it clearly.

"No," she said again. "Not to me. You need to present it to the machine."

"Right." I nodded and held my card up to the screen.

"Not like that," she said. "You need to *present* the card to the machine."

At this point, it became clear to me that the word *present* has a more specific meaning in Australia than it does in America. But she still had to spell it out for me.

"Look," she said. "There's a little slot down here, and you stick your card *into* the machine."

"Oh," I said. The slot was in addition to the regular place where you swipe the card. This added bit of technology, which read the card's security chip, was present in much of the world at the time but hadn't yet reached America, hence my ignorance. I inserted the card.

The attendant sighed. "It's upside down."

It would take me approximately five more tries before I'd figure it out. At least the grocery store was next to Liquor Land.

After Liquor Land, we wandered into a nearby butcher shop and opted for some basic inexpensive meat. I paid with cash, because it seemed one manner in which I could transfer funds without any danger of embarrassing myself. When the butcher handed me my change, he also passed along two, stout little sausages, connected end to end. They were cold and looked like stubby, raw hot dogs in bright red casings. "For your girls," he said and smiled.

I smiled back nervously. "Oh. What . . . what are they?"

"Cheerios," he answered. I made a mental note of this linguistic difference, so that in the future, if someone offered me cheerios, I shouldn't expect a bowl of cereal or anything that might come in a Honey Nut variety.

If someone hands me an unknown fruit or vegetable, I have no problem shoving it in my mouth. But if it's a cold meat product hidden in a casing, I get a little squeamish. Not just of the inner contents but the casing itself. You never know when a casing is edible or when it's something you're supposed to peel off. Well, usually you know it's something you were supposed to peel off once you've put it in your mouth and find that you are masticating in vain and that you will inevitably have to find a way to remove the paper in your mouth with tact, which is not possible.

The butcher was a small man with a gray beard and glasses. He smiled and waited for us to try the cheerios. I tried to hand the sausages to Mike, but my husband pretended at that moment not to have use of his limbs and looked at me with an expression that said, *You're on your own.* I pulled the little sausages apart and handed them to my girls, terrified that they would take a bite and rudely scream *"Ew"* but also equally terrified that they might like and devour this mystery meat. They loved them.

"Thank you," I said. In an effort to apologize for my hesitancy, I added, "We've never had these before."

"Oh!" he said. "Well, in that case, here are some for you too." He retrieved two more from the case and handed them to me.

Don't fear the butcher. Don't fear the butcher. "Thank you," I said, then turned and left so that I wouldn't have to take a bite in front of him.

On the sidewalk out front, Mike and I stood and stared at the sausages in my hand, conscious of the fact that the exceedingly kind butcher could very well still be surveying us through the glass storefront. Mike was as reluctant as I was, which was comforting. It wasn't just my disproportion-ate squeamishness, because Mike has no problem trying the bloodiest of blood pudding or snacking on chicken livers, and heaven to him is gnawing on venison jerky, but even he was shy of these little sausages. Part of the problem was how cold they were and that unmistakable feel of uncooked hot dog. Another detractor was the near neon color of the casing. It didn't look like something that should be ingested. Our kids were gleefully finishing up the last of their sausages and asking for more, which struck me as ironic in light of the fact that they balk at a strawberry with too many seeds.

Later I would return for an entire bag of cheerios, because while I still found them off-putting, our kids loved them. And mystery meat from a butcher shop was likely safer than any number of times when I've let them eat fast food.

Back in Buderim, we unloaded our stock, and Mike imme-diately cracked open a small jar of Vegemite.

"Let's try it," he said enthusiastically. "I've heard so much about it. I can't wait to see what all the fuss is about."

"Okay," I said warily. Vegemite is a curiously popular dark brown paste made from leftover brewers' yeast extract. I had a vague recollection of it at some point in my past. And while I couldn't recall any distinct flavor, I did remember my face contorting in a grimace after only a very small taste.

"I think I'm going to like it," Mike insisted. "Let's try it on toast."

Two minutes later, I looked over to my husband to see him displaying the very same grimace I remembered from my own experience with Vegemite. I took a bite and joined him. It was just as I remembered.

"Oh god," he said. "I was planning on making the kids try

this, but that would be cruel. I don't think I can even finish this piece of toast."

I felt disappointed in myself for not liking it. I wanted to embrace Vegemite, learn to love Vegemite, *be one* with Vegemite. After all, this was an Australian product (though now owned by an American company) found in the vast majority of Australian homes for almost a hundred years. I approached Mike's abandoned toast on the counter and took another nibble, which truly was my last.

* * *

On our second trip to the grocery store, I raced around with Emilia in tow while Mike and Ivy went into the nearby pharmacy to restock our supply of the ever-important bug spray and sunscreen. I searched for bacon but could find it nowhere in the meat department. When I finally asked an employee, she said, "Bacon? It's on the other side of the store in the dairy section." *Silly me*, I thought. *Why would bacon be in the meat department?*

When Mike and Ivy met up with us, I was almost finished shopping but still needed to find canned pumpkin for the pumpkin pie at our upcoming mock-Thanksgiving with Levi and his family.

"I just need to find pumpkin," I said to Mike as he approached. "Wait, where's my wallet?" I searched the cart. I'd been holding my wallet, having left my purse at home. It was nowhere to be seen, and I slowly accepted the reality that I'd set it down somewhere. Driver's license, credit cards, cash, medical insurance card, all of it gone. How would I replace such things in Australia? Paramount was the horror of losing a gift card to the Cheesecake Factory; fate is cruel.

Mike had the disappointed look on his face that screamed "Fail!" and "I can't believe you did that!" and a million other accusatory things that, like a good spouse, he wouldn't give voice to. Instead he said, "Why don't you retrace your steps?"

"Right." I left him with the cart and the kids to retrace my steps, which meant stepping on every square inch of space in the store, as I'd shopped every aisle. I darted around ineffectively before finally approaching an employee at the bakery. "Excuse me," I said. A young man looked at me expectantly. "I feel like I . . ." He looked alarmed, as if I was about to tell him I felt a heart attack coming on. "I mean," I corrected. "I think I set my wallet down somewhere." He looked relieved and directed me to customer service, where I stood in line behind another beautiful surfer, tall and lean and tan, and I mentally listed all the things I could have ordered at the Cheesecake Factory.

"Can I help you?" the clerk asked when it was my turn.

"Yes. I think I set my wallet down somewhere." I cringed at the thought of my own expression, which I knew was wretched and desperate, the outward display of my inner knowledge that the wallet was surely gone.

"Right," he said. "This you?" He held up my wallet, opened so I could glance at the license picture inside, and handed it over.

A quick look told me that the credit cards, cash, and beloved gift card were still present. I looked up at the clerk.

"*Thank you,*" I said, with such force that he took a step back and looked thankful that a counter was between us, lest I try to physically communicate my thanks.

I beamed when I returned to Mike, whose shoulders relaxed when he saw me in possession of my wallet.

"Let's get out of here," he said.

"Agreed."

I never located pumpkin for our pseudo Thanksgiving and instead made a gloppy but delicious chocolate concoction. When we arrived at Levi's home for the feast, I handed over my messy chocolate goodness and explained, "I made this instead because I couldn't find canned pumpkin."

"Oh, yeah. You're not going to find *canned* pumpkin in any of the grocery stores here," Levi said.

"Oh, so you thought I was going to make pumpkin pie from a real pumpkin?" This was both hilarious and adorable, but that's what you get when your husband tells people you can make *anything*.

Thanksgiving felt exactly like a Thanksgiving in the United States, except we routinely applied sunscreen and bug spray and ate outside on their deck while the kids played in a kiddie pool. In the absence of our own extended family, it was wonderful to be in the presence of Levi and his family, whom I found to be the perfect example of joyful living and a conscious avoidance of drama. All of which enhanced the gratitude of the day itself.

When we returned to Buderim that evening, Emilia commanded me to sit on the couch.

"Just wait right there, Mama, and *don't peek.*"

"Okay," I agreed, shutting my eyes.

"Dad," she said in her signature loud whisper. "Where are the cards?"

"Right here."

I knew, in part because I am The Mom and in part because Emilia's whisper is so deafening, that Mike had instructed the girls to make Thanksgiving cards for me while he took an hour of homeschool duty the day before.

"Okay, Mom," Emilia said.

"Open your eyes," Ivy added.

They stood in front of me, each holding a homemade card of folded paper and crayon that read, "Happy Thanksgiving Mom."

I gave the requisite oohs and ahhs of appreciation and hugged them both.

"Wait. Now you sit down, Dad," Emilia commanded, and took the cards back from me. He did so, and we heard Emilia's instructions to her sister. "Come on, Ivy. I have a plan."

We sat with our eyes closed for a full minute before we heard them shuffle back into place before us.

"Okay, Dad," Emilia said.

"Open your eyes," Ivy barked.

He did so, and they presented him with the same cards they'd given me a minute before, though this time with the addition of "and Dad" under "Happy Thanksgiving Mom."

"Wow, girls," Mike said. "Thank you. I feel so special."

* * *

The next day, we returned to Mooloolaba, this time taking with us a boogie board we'd found in the hall closet. I couldn't picture the Artiste boogie boarding and assumed it was there for the benefit of grandkids, who would neither mind nor know if we borrowed it. I had no intention of going in the water, but Emilia wanted to "surf." It only took her a few successful instances of boogie boarding on a previous trip to a beach in the United States before she began confidently describing herself as a surfer to anyone who would listen. In Mooloolaba, as she headed into the water, I could tell she had to restrain herself from approaching every stranger there and saying, "Watch me! I'm going to surf!"

Emilia's fairly competent in the water, but her elevated confidence often scares me. And while I love to watch the joy on her face when she catches a good wave, I am constantly on edge as she travels farther out into the water, crashes into an unsuspecting couple and what might have been a romantic moment, or drifts down the shore, unaware that she's once again traveled far outside of the lifeguard's territory.

"I'll get this one," Mike said in reference to an instance of the latter. He walked down the beach, got her attention, and once again pointed to the lifeguard flags from which she'd strayed. She dutifully trudged back to the safe zone before embarking out again.

"Ivy, do you want to go play in the water?" Mike asked. "I'll go with you." There was optimism in his voice, the hope that she might want to get exercise, enjoy the natural beauty of the beach and sea, or embrace a spirit of adventure.

In such situations, however, Ivy leans more in my direction. She turned to me and asked, "Do we have any snacks?"

When we returned to Buderim, some of us having snacked more than "surfed," we realized we'd left the boogie board behind. A boogie board that wasn't ours and that would cost about forty dollars to replace. I could picture it sitting near the spigot where we'd rinsed off our feet before getting back in the car. Closing my eyes, I summoned the image of it, convincing myself I could remember the exact picture of dolphins on the front when we would later go shopping to replace it.

"I'm going to drive back to get it," Mike stated.

"What?" I opened my eyes. "All the way to Mooloolaba?"

"Yes."

"It's okay, Mike. We'll just replace it. We'll buy another one."

"I'm going back for it."

"It's probably not still sitting there."

"I just feel like that's the right thing to do."

"Okay," I said, though I disagreed. It was surely gone, and if Mike spent forty minutes driving to retrieve a phantom boogie board, he would be in less than good humor by the time he returned, so as soon as he left, I readied the ingredients for a stiff drink. He'd need it.

Mike returned forty minutes later—with the boogie board.

"You're kidding," I said.

"Nope." He smiled.

"Why is everyone here so *kind?*" I asked.

"I guess that's just Australia."

* * *

The Crocoseum

Crikey: (cri·key, /ˈkrīkē/)
An expression of surprise. Mid 19th century: euphemism for Christ.

– Oxford Dictionary

As welcomed as we felt in Australia, we couldn't mooch forever. Eventually Levi and his wife needed their car back, so we rented a vehicle from a private party near Brisbane for our remaining weeks on the Sunshine Coast, before we moved into the camper van.

"You know this means you'll have to drive," Mike said.

"I can drive," I confirmed.

"Of course Mama can drive," Emilia backed me up.

"Mom, did you forget how to drive?" Ivy asked.

"I can drive," I asserted again.

I'd have to leave the comfort zone of the passenger seat for us to retrieve the rental car and drive both cars to Levi's home in Coolum, so that we could hand over the keys and once again return to being a one-car family.

"How come you haven't driven in Australia?" Emilia asked.

"Because Daddy prefers to drive," I said. "And he needs me to navigate," I added.

"You mean to be his Keep Lefter?" Ivy asked, referring to my constant reminder to "keep left, keep left."

"Exactly!"

There was no reason for me to think that I couldn't handle driving on the other side of the road from the other side of the car just like countless tourists and travelers had done before me. But my apprehension remained, that fear that if I did cause an accident, my humiliation would be unbearable, and I would ruin the trip and therefore the lives of everyone involved.

We drove down the M1 to an apartment just south of Brisbane in Kippa-Ring. I was thankful to get a peek into the apartment complex because our cushy accommodations in Buderim had me thinking that every Australian lived in a white hilltop palace or beachfront bungalow. This was a typical apartment complex like you might see in America, and the young couple who lived there (and often rented their second car for extra cash) greeted us at the door.

"Hi," I said.

"Hello," said a twenty-something male. "Come on in." We all shuffled in to handle the paperwork of the rental agreement. The tiny apartment was cluttered with DVDs and books, mostly sci-fi, and a large terrarium occupied one wall.

"Girls," I commanded, "please don't touch anything."

"Oh, it's okay," said the man. "They can hold the lizard."

Normally I might bristle when a man I don't know offers his lizard for my daughters to hold, but Australia had earned certain allowances with me. He retrieved a bearded dragon from the terrarium. It was a prehistoric-looking creature with spiny scales that were unexpectedly soft to the touch, the type of creature that makes some people cringe but which I find adorable. I supervised the children, more for the lizard's safety than my daughters', while Mike and the car owner spent ten minutes trading information and initialing various boxes. The process, through an online site that matches private owners willing to rent their vehicles to would-be renters, was fairly straightforward and far cheaper than if we'd used a typical car rental business. And it is the cumulative effect of savings like these and home exchanges and airline mile redemption that make extended travel for a family like ours (of moderate means as opposed to excessive wealth) possible.

We bade the bearded dragon farewell and traded him to his owner in exchange for the car keys. I would drive the rental (an automatic) and Mike would continue driving Levi's car.

"Do you want me to take the girls? Or one of the girls?" I asked Mike.

He stood with a serious look on his face before asserting, "I want the girls to ride with me."

I believe there were two reasons for this. One was that our girls, when riding in the back of a car, can become either combative with each other or overly friendly. In either case, they can be a distraction. As it would be my first experience driving in Australia, on the other side of the road and from the other side of the car, Mike didn't want me to have to contend with those distractions. The second reason he wanted the kids to ride with him was that if I died in a fiery crash, at least he wouldn't lose his whole family.

I followed Mike for the one-hour return trip, constantly checking my side mirrors to make sure I was where I thought I was, and mistakenly turning on the windshield wipers every time I meant to use the turn signal. The wiper blade mistake occurred approximately one million times. I wasn't annoyed by the mix-up but by the fact that I continued making it, over and over again. If you ever see someone's wipers employed for no apparent reason, you should give them some space and understanding. They're likely adjusting to an unfamiliar orientation of steering wheel, lane direction, and turn signal lever.

I had no working cell phone in Australia. This shouldn't be a big deal, because it wasn't that long ago when no one had a cell phone, and I'm amazed at how quickly we've become dependent and addicted to the ability to attempt to contact anyone at any time. I didn't feel much panic at my lack of phone in Australia. It felt like the return of a freedom, one I hadn't realized had been taken away. The exception was driving alone on the Australian freeway, attempting to tailgate my husband so as not to lose him. Because what would I do if we were separated? I certainly didn't know where to go. Even if I had directions, I'd surely get lost. I'm severely challenged when it comes to orienting myself in the world or navigating anywhere even the slightest bit unfamiliar. To mitigate my fear, we traveled with walkie-talkies. Fully charged and ready for my distress call in case I suddenly started driving on the incorrect, but right, side of the road. The walkie-talkies were there for safety, though they inevitably led to repeated utterances of "Breaker, breaker" or attempts at talking dirty.

"What are you wearing?" Mike asked in a low voice.

"My gray cargo shorts and a stained T-shirt," I answered. "Why?"

"Yeah," he called back. "You suck at this."

"I know. Over and out."

We made it safely back to Coolum where we returned Levi's vehicle and I relinquished the driver's seat of our rented car. I'm pleased to report that at no point in the journey did I die in a fiery crash.

After dropping off Levi's car, Mike suggested we check out Noosa Heads.

"It's a hundred degrees, and you want to go to the beach?" I asked incredulously. Extreme heat makes me want to hunker down inside, while Mike instinctively searches for water, which I might also do if I didn't hate water.

"It'll be cooler there. I promise."

The heat had zapped my will to fight, so I sat silently as he drove to Noosa, where we saw every other inhabitant of the Sunshine Coast also looking for a parking spot. The congestion of traffic combined with the heat added a note of hostility to the air, born of impatience and frustration. Mike pulled into a parking lot, one that we could easily see had no spots to offer. Drivers perched like predators waiting for a space to open so that they could move in for the kill. A minute later, we found ourselves in a narrow lane with a line of cars approaching us.

"Mike, this is one way," I blurted. "Retreat, retreat!"

"You know, we've got two sets of eyes here," he snapped, handing me my half of the blame as failed navigator. The problem was the situation was already stressful, and when the situation is stressful, I am a complete failure as a copilot. I want nothing more than to stick my head in the sand (figuratively, of course, because . . . sand), and two sets of eyes are hardly more effective than one when one set is cowering and waiting for the storm to pass.

Eventually we found a parking spot, far away from the main area we'd hoped to reach. We made our way to the beach and walked along to where we'd initially hoped to be, and I grudgingly admitted to Mike that he was right; it was much cooler there. The natural beauty of Noosa was in its incomparable landscape, with the pronounced contrast of green forest, white beach, and turquoise waters fading out into blue. There were surfers and kayakers and beach loungers but with space enough for everyone. And I realized that one of the things I'd always detested about a day at the beach was feeling confined to the space of a beach towel while dealing with a neighbor's music, trash, dog, and/or offensive conversation. Not that I don't like people. I'm just drawn to sitting next to the wrong ones. But Noosa had none of that, and I gradually came to realize that my impression of a beach could be more like this one and less like an image of the Jersey Shore on the Fourth of July.

The temperature dropped even further from sweltering as we walked along a partially shaded trail in the Noosa National Park, which winds through the forest but still borders the popular beach area, surrounding us with stunning but contrasting views on either side. We'd heard that the trail was a popular trek for spotting koalas in the wild. Before setting out on our hike, we stopped in at the ranger station, only to learn that there hadn't been any koala sightings as of late. This did not dampen my excitement but only made it more thrilling when I would, I was sure, be the first of our party to spot a koala.

I missed much of the beautiful view along the walk and moved at a snail's pace because I studied the trees intently as we made our way along the path, determined to find a nesting koala.

"Oh my gosh." I stopped in my tracks. "Look at that!"

"What is it, Mom?" Emilia asked excitedly.

"It's a—"

"It's a growth on a tree," Mike interjected. I could tell he wanted to interrupt before I blurted out that it was a koala, because the devastation of telling the girls there was a koala, only to then retract the statement, would not be pretty.

"Yeah." My shoulders slumped. "It sure is. It's a tree growth."

We continued along the coastal track past gorgeous views and lookouts with names like Boiling Pot and Hell's Gates, all the way to Alexandria Bay where the immaculate sand made a pleasing squeaking sound with every step. We'd later learn that this is a popular but informal nudist beach, though on the occasion of our visit, we were spared the introduction to any strangers with parts on display. The hike there and back was not a short one, especially for young children, and I was proud of us for completing it with minimal complaining, no snacks, and only one instance of holding a squatting child in the bushes so that she might have a quick pee.

We finished the hike without having spotted a koala and rewarded the kids with an ice-cream cone back at the ranger station before relinquishing our parking spot and making the drive from Noosa back to Buderim, which had me contemplating some of the names of Australian towns. I didn't think I could ever live in Mooloolaba, because as fun as it is to say (once you learn how to do so), between the "moo" and the "laba" I end up with the phrase "cow's labia" in my head, which is not what I want knocking around in my brain. If you're lucky enough to live on the Sunshine Coast, why not live in a place with a name like Beerwah or Sippy Downs? Or even cooler, Coolum? Noosa, as beautiful a spot as it is, brings me to lynching. Murdering Creek needs little explanation, though this name stands as a reminder of the atrocities visited upon Australia's indigenous people, much like white America's own horrific past.

Debates regarding different versions of the history of colonial Australia continue, with politicians and scholars divided on the "Black Armband" version of history, which seeks to acknowledge the exploitation of and violence against Indigenous Australians, versus the "Three Cheers View," which focuses on the positive view of history and opposes dwelling on a negative past. Celebrating achievements is wonderful and necessary, but the history of white settlers' treatment of native people in either the United States or Australia has never brought a "hip, hip, hooray" to my lips. Please pass the armband.

* * *

Before arriving in Australia, I knew we'd be on the Sunshine Coast and not far from Australia Zoo on Steve Irwin Day. This is a day once a year when the zoo celebrates the life and work of Steve Irwin, or as many knew him, the Crocodile Hunter. I'd long been a fan of Steve Irwin and believe I shed more than a few tears when I learned of his death, which is one of those odd situations when you find yourself crying over the single death of someone you never met, yet you can then read the news of the deaths of thousands of people you've never met, through war or natural disaster or shameful history, and quickly and coldly process the information (hip, hip, hooray) before continuing on with your day. But Steve Irwin's wide eyes, mop of hair, and enthusiasm made me feel he was a true friend. He just hadn't known it.

"Tomorrow is Steve Irwin Day at Australia Zoo," I said to Mike.

This began the battle that we periodically wage. When something really cool is about to happen, our first instinct is to talk ourselves out of going. It's not that we don't want to have fun. It's that we have a deep aversion to crowds of people.

"It'll probably be really crowded," Mike said.

"You're right. We should go another time," I agreed.

But our first inclination didn't sit well with me. And after a few minutes, it apparently didn't sit well with Mike, either.

"You know what? We should go," he said.

"You're right. We traveled all the way here, and we're not going to go to Australia Zoo on Steve Irwin Day? That's crazy talk. We're going."

The morning of, I packed Emilia's zebra-print backpack with water, sunscreen, and paper towels. I didn't have any specific use in mind for the paper towels, but motherhood compels women to have some sort of absorbent material on hand at all times. Because in a family with young children, someone will likely leak a bodily fluid at some point.

We arrived at the zoo fairly early, with temperatures already creeping toward flaming hot, otherwise known as a mere thirty-something degrees in Australia. Celsius, like driving, was another way in which I tried to switch my brain to a new manner of thinking, a new system of thought, though I never quite succeeded.

Once we made our way into the park, where I was surprised to see an absence of overwhelming crowds (after all, this was *Steve Irwin* Day), we entered an area where zoo staff held a variety of animals for visitors to learn about, and of course prod. One of the first people we approached held a small American alligator named Hank. I was worried for Ivy's sake. She's been known to run screaming from a small, fluffy puppy, so I feared that the alligator would bring on a fit of terror. On the other hand, she'd been ecstatic, with no hint of fear, upon meeting the bearded dragon in Kippa-Ring. She looked at the alligator, walked up to it, and reached for its head.

"Like this," the handler instructed. "You can touch him along his tail." The handler presented the tail and moved the head away from my daughter's hand, but Ivy simply repositioned herself so that she could once again put her hands as close to the alligator's mouth as possible. The handler kept trying to get Ivy to focus on the tail and eventually resorted to standing up straight and holding the animal's head high, so that the only thing Ivy could reach was the tail, because for some reason my five-year-old really wanted to see if she could get the reptile to bite off her fingers.

We moved on then to an echidna, which would surprisingly emerge as the Australian animal to win my heart. It looked like a hedgehog on steroids. Much larger and with quills soft to the touch as long you pet the animal the right way, which it didn't seem to mind as it sat munching on a mushy mixture of worms and grain.

We made our way throughout the zoo, eventually coming to a small grove of eucalyptus trees where koalas huddled. Signs on the trees told you which koalas you could touch and which ones were to be left alone, and I felt bad for the animals, who didn't appear to enjoy, but rather tolerated, the constant flow of tourists stopping to scratch them on the butt. My earlier dreams of cuddling with the animal until eventually I would have to tear myself away, because it wouldn't want me to leave and would cling to me for more affection, were shattered. I imagined how humans might feel if roles were reversed. How would we adapt to daily life if every five minutes a koala began scratching us on the rear? My desire to interact with a koala gave way to a greater wish that these animals be left alone. Despite the koalas' understandable annoyance, they were still cuter than tree growths.

As we moved on to the next exhibit, we stopped in the middle of a pathway.

"Holy crap," I said. A giant, exotic bird stood in front of us. "I think somebody got out of his cage!" I was contemplating finding zoo staff to alert them to this escapee when I saw a giant, exotic lizard on the pavement next to the bird.

"Whoa, look at that!" Mike said.

"Oh my god, are all the animals escaping? Has someone let them loose? This will not end well!"

"Calm down," Mike said.

"Don't tell me to calm down. I read *Setting Free the Bears!*"

"What?"

"Curse your limited knowledge of early John Irving novels!"

"No one is setting free any bears. This zoo doesn't even have bears."

"They have koala bears," Ivy said.

"But those aren't *really* bears," Emilia corrected.

At that point, a couple with a child about Emilia's age walked up. The son said, "Look, Mummy. A bush turkey."

"Yes, darling," Mummy replied, with as much enthusiasm as I have for the NFL. Her reaction told me that this was not something to worry about. The lizard appeared to have the same effect on them as a squirrel does on me in the United States. Basically, I just try not to run over them.

The Australian family moved on while we, like true tourists, stood fascinated by these freely roaming animals.

"Let me get your picture," Mike said.

"Okay." I stood near the lizard.

"I can only get your feet. Crouch down there next to it."

I knelt on the path.

"Lower," Mike advised. "Get your face down there next to it so I can get you both in the shot."

I crouched down as far as I could and lowered my face near the pavement, at which point my butt was higher than my head, which caused the zebra-print backpack I'd been carting around, heavy with water bottles, to slide the length of my back and clock me in the back of the head. I tried to keep smiling, despite growing annoyance, but the lizard may have been startled by my proximity as well as the sudden movement of the backpack and darted at my nose. The weight of the backpack still pressing on the back of my head, combined with flinching from the lunging lizard, caused me to topple over to the side. My family attempted not to laugh at me as I stood, took the camera from Mike, and vowed not to pose for any further pictures.

In the coming weeks, we'd see the bush turkeys (also known as brushturkeys) on front lawns, in forests, and in the parking lot of the grocery store. Like the lizards and macaws and fruit bats, they were simply part of the local landscape. With each spotting, Mike would quietly muse, "I wonder how they taste."

We entered an immense area where red and gray kangaroos lounged, fat and happy in the shade, nibbling the roo food that visitors purchased in nearby vending machines. The zoo calls this habitat an open-range enclosure; it was open and expansive enough, with variances in terrain and winding paths, that you could easily forget it was an enclosure of any kind.

"How about this one, Mom?" Emilia pointed to a kangaroo.

"Okay, I guess so." The animals were docile and calm but still very large, and we had no knowledge of how to properly approach them, so we did so tentatively. We gently fed and petted the kangaroo before moving on.

"How about this one?" Ivy indicated another kangaroo.

A khaki-clad staff member stood nearby. "Actually," he said, "this one needs a little space right now."

"Okay," Ivy said, and we moved on. I was thankful for the presence of staff and some effort to allow the animals respite from our attentions, should they need it.

Because it was Steve Irwin Day, the Crocodile Hunter's widow, Terri, and children, Bindi and Robert, were present and put on a special memorial tribute in a large arena known as the Crocoseum. I was excited about the show and for the chance to sit in the shade. The heat was debilitating, and I found myself constantly scanning those around me, family and strangers alike, to make sure no one had passed out.

The show included the usual presentation and feeding of crocodiles with a good mix of implied danger and overt humor.

To mark the special occasion, they also brought in a singer to perform, and psychic Jon Edwards. Both of these troubled me. The singer, a young American who flew in that morning, was clad in the signature Australia Zoo khaki, perched on a large platform high in the Crocoseum, and proceeded to put on a mini concert in the stifling heat. We sat in the shade, barely surviving, and I couldn't imagine how the singer made it through, belting Beyoncé's "Halo." If he passed out from heat exhaustion, he'd likely topple from the platform and fall into the crocodile pond. Then we'd *really* have a show.

The singer survived, and it was Jon Edwards's turn to speak. I cringed. If he channeled Steve Irwin there in the stadium while standing next to his widow and children, I feared I might throw up in my lap. But he didn't. Instead he spoke tastefully and respectfully of Irwin, who had apparently been a friend. When Terri, the Crocodile Hunter's widow, spoke, shadowed by her teenage daughter and preteen son, I felt an odd sensation in my throat and chest, which I attributed to the heat. Then my eyes began to water. I looked around. No one else was crying, but there I was getting choked up. And no matter how much they tried to praise the legacy and work of Irwin, and to make the day a celebration, I could do nothing but fall apart at the thought of his death. I discretely retrieved the paper towels from the zebra backpack and dabbed at my eyes, turning away from Mike and the girls.

After the show, as we exited the Crocoseum, Emilia declared, "Now we need to go see some *real* crocodiles."

"Emilia, those were real crocodiles," Mike said.

"Yeah, but I want to go to the place where we can wrestle them."

"There isn't any place here where you can wrestle crocodiles," I said. "There isn't any place *anywhere* where you can wrestle crocodiles. Please don't ever try to wrestle a crocodile."

"Yes, there is. I saw it. It's right over here."

She led us to a lawn where an employee demonstrated crocodile roping on a soft and cuddly thirty-foot-long replica of the animal.

"Well, okay," I said. "You can wrestle that crocodile."

The employee instructed Emilia to rope the jaw and Ivy to tackle it. They took turns vigorously subduing the massive stuffed animal.

"How are they doing that without completely passing out?" Mike asked.

"I don't know," I answered, ineffectively fanning myself with my hand. "I feel like I'm going to pass out just standing here."

"Come on, girls," Mike beckoned. "Let's move on."

"Okay," Ivy chirped as she dismounted the crocodile. "Let's go see some more *real* crocodiles." At that, they led us to a giant, kid-friendly, and climbable statue of prehistoric crocodiles in mortal combat with a dinosaur. I didn't understand why, after watching the presentation of real crocodiles, they were determined to search out fake ones and call them real. Maybe they were willing to sacrifice reality if it meant they could mount the creatures. Or perhaps it was that most maddening of days, Opposite Day, in which I have never found any enjoyment.

"We should go soon," I said to Mike.

"What about the wombat?"

"I think we'll have to pass," I said. "It's just so hot." I could feel our collective life force dwindling by the second.

"Are you sure? You've been talking about how much you want to see a wombat for months."

"I'm sure we'll have other opportunities," I said. "I think we should go before they melt."

As we exited, we again passed through the animal handlers near the front entrance, who had since rotated with a new set of animals. A man held a giant golden boa constrictor decorated in dark brown patterns. The girls ran to him.

"Wow! What's his name?" Emilia asked.

"This is Ricky," said the handler.

Ivy reached to pet the snake on the head, and the handler performed the same evasive tactics as the alligator handler had upon our arrival.

"What kind of snake is he?"

"He's a boa constrictor."

"And what's his name?" Emilia asked again.

"What is it?" Ivy asked.

"It's a boa constrictor."

"What is his name?"

"Ricky! His name is Ricky!" The handler moved in circles, trying to evade Ivy, who was relentless in her pursuit of the animal's head and appeared not to hear any of us warn her away from it. Eventually I picked her up, which seemed the only way to break her of the compelling desire to touch a reptile in the face, and we headed toward the exit.

Regardless of Steve Irwin's celebrity and not because of it, the Australia Zoo was a fantastic zoo. I'm not a fan of imprisoning wildlife, but their conservation and rehabilitation efforts are both considerable and commendable. And if you are an animal and you have to be in a zoo, I'm convinced the Australia Zoo is the one you want. As far as the girls were concerned, the real (fake) crocodiles were the highlight of the day.

"I love that place," Ivy said in the parking lot.

"When I grow up, I want to work there," Emilia added.

By the time we reached Buderim, euphoria had given way to cranky exhaustion. I figured a quick and easy dinner was in order and promised to give the children hot dogs, because overly processed meat products on overly processed baked goods make them happy. But when I retrieved the "hot dogs" Mike had picked out at the grocery store, I realized they were yet another version of creepy little sausages. These weren't precooked sausages that just needed to be reheated. They were raw meat encased in whatever odd substance is used to make sausage casing, which I'm pretty sure is the same material used to create Spanx. The more I cooked them, the creepier they got, and when I nibbled one, I knew for sure that I wouldn't be feeding them to my kids.

"You know, girls, these sausages aren't very good. I don't think we're going to eat them, after all."

"But can we still have these?" Ivy asked, holding up the bag of cheap, white hot-dog buns.

"Yes," I answered. "Yes, you can." Feeding my children white hot-dog buns for dinner made me feel less than fantastic in the motherhood department. But maybe that was better than if those buns had contained the creepy sausages. And really, what is sausage casing made of? Contemplating sausage casings reminded me of a dreaded but necessary chore in my near future: swimsuit shopping.

*   *   *

Humping the Dingo

I am not the sort of woman who would wear high heels with a bathing suit. Let's get that straight right now.

—Vera Wang

Homeschooling had long been one of those things I dreaded. I adore my kids, but the thought of spending all day every day with them terrifies me, which then makes me feel like a terrible person and a shitty mom (hot-dog bun, anyone?). I gave homeschooling my all, despite the fact that every day involved Emilia dissolving into tears and running back to bed. I recognized this as nothing more than the difficulty of learning something from someone you love, which is why it's also never a good idea to learn skiing or any kind of sport from your spouse. At least if you want to stay married. But there are plenty of people out there who are very successful at homeschooling, so I knew we'd survive. Part of the problem may have been that Emilia's homework seemed daunting when compared to Ivy's kindergarten curriculum. While trying to explain math concepts to Emilia, her younger sister's assignments often amounted to little more than color by number. Frustration is normal, though

I often wondered where the intensity of her distress came from, and I marveled at how quickly it could escalate.

Another component of our new circumstances was privacy. I ached to have a moment alone. Traveling with your family for months on end takes away the usual bits of your routine that you enjoy on your own. When I had the kids working on material that they could complete themselves, without tears, and that would take at least ten minutes, I quietly grabbed my book and slipped out to the deck. It's worth noting that this instance was a rarity when it came to schoolwork. I learned early and the hard way that if we were to make any academic progress during our time abroad, my children needed my full attention and engagement. Homeschooling is destined for failure if you give half-assed instructions while checking your e-mail, especially when dealing with elementary school-aged students. But the rare ten minutes presented themselves, and I jumped on the opportunity. I'd been seated for a few seconds and had just found the page where I'd left off when the sliding glass door opened and Emilia and Ivy walked over and stood in front of me.

"What are you guys doing?" I asked.

"We didn't want you to be alone," Emilia said, and patted my shoulder as if in consolation. You'd never have guessed she'd screamed at me twenty minutes prior for trying to assist her in calculating how many cupcakes Jane would have if she started with thirty and ate eleven. And who cared, really? The more important question is: Will Jane get the help she needs to address her critical and unhealthy relationship with high-fructose corn syrup?

"You know," I told the girls, "sometimes adults actually *like* to be alone."

"Why?" Ivy asked with a look of horror.

"We just do." I smiled, and I could tell she didn't believe me. I gave up on the book.

When we'd finished our lessons and Mike had put in a few hours of work on the computer, we considered our options for getting out of the house in the afternoon.

"Mooloolaba again?" Mike asked. "Or would you rather try a different beach?"

To me, every grain of sand is a reason not to go to the beach, no matter how breathtaking the landscape, but you can't visit a place like Australia and turn your nose up at such things. At the same time, we'd spent just about every afternoon at one beach or another. And while that might sound like a dream to many people, it's not mine. I also didn't want to go to the beach because then I'd once again be confronted by the fact that I needed to buy a new bathing suit. Both Noosa and Mooloolaba offered countless stores with swimwear, but the horrors of swimsuit shopping seemed too much to handle, so I pushed for a walk through the market in Eumundi (yoo-MUN-dee), a town whose name is pleasing enough that I decided I *could* live there.

"Well, okay," Mike relented. But I could tell he didn't see the logic in not going to the beach when we had the opportunity to do so. It was a short drive to Eumundi. As soon as we approached the market, I could tell that this was not your typical farmers' market but a sprawling artisan's nirvana. The first path we chose turned out to be the spiritual one, with psychics and masseuses giving readings and massages in curtained outdoor rooms. The food vendors looked to be on a gourmet scale. And while I don't consider myself an enthusiastic shopper, I could easily have spent a few thousand dollars there on art, clothing, and jewelry. Mike wandered ahead and found a stall he was apparently interested in while I trailed with the girls, trying to cultivate more of an interest in the hand-carved, wooden toys than the *Frozen* dresses (not all the wares were of the artisan variety).

By the time we finally reached Mike, I was curious to see what had piqued his interest, and was then instantly dismayed to find that he stood in front of a stall selling lingerie and bikinis. I'd thought that in not going to the beach I could delay the inevitable and dreaded swimsuit shopping, but there was no escape. At least not as long as we were on the east coast of mainland Australia, which boasts swimsuits aplenty.

"Look, honey," Mike said, obviously pleased with himself. "They have swimsuits here."

"Yeah." I nodded. The bikinis were very cute but didn't seem to include much fabric. "It's a shame there's nowhere to try them on. I'm not buying a bathing suit without trying it on first."

"She has a spot for you to try them on." He motioned to the stall owner, who appeared to be about twenty years of age and no doubt would look exceedingly hot in any of the lingerie or suits she was selling.

"I make these all myself," she said. "And of course you can try anything on right here." She had a small area curtained off in the back corner of her stall. It made me feel a little vulnerable, until I considered all of the people we'd passed who were getting full-body massages in curtained areas only slightly bigger than this one.

I entered the makeshift changing room, and Mike passed me a handful of tops and bottoms. The benefit of changing in such a tiny space is that you can't actually step back and get a full view of yourself. I've reached the point in life when I am past wasting energy on feeling body shame, but that doesn't mean I want to stare at half-naked me in a mirror, either.

I'd removed my dress and had a bikini in place when Emilia swept back the curtain and Ivy proclaimed, "Mama, you look beautiful!"

My daughters tell me I look beautiful in virtually any state. It does not matter what I am plagued by at the moment, be it acne, body odor, or hair that vermin could nest in. And while this is sweet and endearing, I did not want the thousand people in attendance at the Eumundi market witnessing me in a bikini.

"Thank you, girls!" I said, and quickly closed the curtain. I was thankful that the curtains were thick enough to keep me from feeling even more on display than I already did. At the same time, the small space intensified the already blazing heat of the afternoon, and I figured it probably wouldn't matter how I looked in my new bikini if I suffocated to death.

"Just me." Mike opened the curtain half an inch to steal a peek. "Yeah, I think you should definitely get that one. Here, try this one on." He passed another one into my tiny tent.

"Uh, okay. But one is probably enough."

"Nah, I think you need more than one."

My husband has never been a cheapskate when it comes to skimpy clothing. One year for Christmas he bought me a fluffy, pink bathrobe. I thought it uncharacteristic of him to buy me an item of clothing that typically hides the body. Until I put it on and found it to be so short that it barely covered my ass, at which point he proclaimed that it fit perfectly.

"How's it going?" Mike asked as I tried on the second bikini.

"Okay," I said, starting to sweat. "But I'm having trouble with the clasp." He reached in and clasped the back of the top just as Ivy hoisted up the bottom of the curtain.

"Ooh!" Ivy yelled.

"Pretty!" Emilia concurred.

"Hey!" I was losing my patience, and as much as I wanted to graciously accept their compliments, the vulnerability that comes with standing in a bikini and having someone pull back the curtains was maddening. "Mike, can you please stop them from doing that."

"Of course, sweetie." I then heard him explain to them for a full minute how people need privacy sometimes. "You know, like when they change their clothes or go to the bathroom or take a bath. Sometimes people just need a little space."

"Or when you and Mama are naked together," Emilia added.

"Sometimes I talk to Mom while she poops," Ivy declared, with more volume than I would have hoped for.

"Right now, Mom needs a little space, so I'd like you two to stand right over here," he said.

I relaxed a little until the curtain unexpectedly parted again. This time Mike's head poked through. "So, how's it going? Yeah, you should get that one too. Want me to find more?"

"No," I said. "I'm done. Now get out of here." I palmed his face, pushed it back through the curtains, and drew them closed, wishing there was a way to lock them. All I wanted was to get back into my dress and escape the oppressive heat of the dressing room. But as difficult as it had been to get the bikini top on, getting it off was more so. I peeked through the curtain myself.

"Do you need help?" Mike asked and started coming toward me.

"No," I barked. "You stay with the girls." I then adopted a more polite tone. "Excuse me," I said to the hot, young talent who created the clothing and ran the business. "Can you help me? I'm having trouble getting this off."

"Of course," she said.

She entered the tiny curtained area and wrestled with the back clasp. I'd decided that I didn't need a suit that I couldn't put on and take off by myself, but as her hands touched my back, which was dripping with sweat, I felt bad for sweating in her handmade suit. I felt bad for anyone else who would have to wear a suit that housed my sweaty boobs. It felt like the equivalent of: you break it, you buy it. I'd sweated in the suit to such an extent that I had no other recourse than to hand over my credit card.

With the swimsuit shopping mercifully behind us, we walked to the shade of a nearby playground on the outskirts of the market. It was shaded with magnificent trees, and not once in the hundreds of pictures I took was I ever able to capture that magnificence. The girls gleefully played on the playground while Mike and I sat and chatted. It's easy to keep track of your children on a busy playground when they speak in an accent different from that of all the other children. But at one point, I didn't hear them anymore.

"I see Emilia," I said to Mike. "But where's Ivy?"

"She's . . . uh . . . humping the dingo." Mike pointed across the playground to where Ivy furiously rocked back and forth on a piece of equipment that appeared to be a ride replica of a dingo.

"Well, as long as it's consensual."

We made one last pass through the market, stopping briefly at a stand selling ginger beer.

"This is the finest ginger beer you'll find!" the vendor boomed. "Here, have a sample."

"You're very enthusiastic," I said.

"Yes, I am!"

"Mike, come have a sample of ginger beer with me."

"Okay. What's the alcohol content of this?" Mike asked.

"Very little," he assured us. "Trace amounts, and it would be all right for the children, if that's why you ask."

"No," Mike said, "I wasn't worried about that."

"We actually wanted it to be *more* alcoholic," I clarified. "But I guess we could always add vodka to it."

"Oh," he smiled. "Yes, you could certainly do that. And add some mint, and you've got a Moscow mule."

I hadn't been that impressed with the ginger beer, nor had any intention of buying a bottle until its potential as a mixer came to light.

"Ooh, you know what else we should buy?" I said to Mike as he paid for the ginger beer. "They'd make great souvenirs to give. We should buy a bunch of . . . oh, what do you call them . . . budgy smugglers!" I'd been trying to gain some grasp of Australian slang, and I was referring to what in the States are known as beer cozies (or koozies, depending on what part of the country you're in). Everyone has them in Australia because of the heat, and they were often sold as good, cheap souvenirs. But the ginger beer vendor shifted uncomfortably at my mention of buying everyone budgy smugglers. Was that considered tacky? I thought of a handful of friends back home who would love an Australian budgy smuggler, until I realized I'd confused my slang. I'd meant to say *stubby cooler*, which was Aussie slang for beer cozy. Unfortunately, the cadence of stubby cooler is similar to budgy smuggler, and so

I'd confused the two and loudly announced that we should buy a bunch of men's Speedos (or "banana hammocks," as it were) for our friends back home.

"When do *we* get to buy something?" Emilia asked.

We'd done fairly well in letting the kids know that they couldn't have everything they wanted, that things cost money, and that it was annoying to adults to constantly be asked by kids to buy them things. Since we'd spent money on bikinis and mixers for alcohol, it felt like the right thing to do to buy a *little* something for the kids. And since they are still young enough to think that dollar toys are fantastic, that's what we gravitated toward. One of the stands sold cheap toys, and one of those toys was a "kangaroo egg," the type of thing you put in water and watch hatch and grow.

"I didn't think kangaroos came out of eggs," Emilia said.

"They don't," I clarified.

"So, we'll have a real baby kangaroo?" Ivy asked.

"No, Ivy," her sister answered. "We're going to have a real baby chicken."

"There will be no real baby animal," I insisted.

"I've always wanted a pet," Ivy said.

Their excitement over a potential pet trumped any logic or clarification I might offer. We've explained on many occasions why we don't have pets, mainly because that would prohibit travel to the extent that we undertake it.

"But why can't we have a kitten?" Emilia asked on a prior discussion of the pet conundrum.

"If we had a kitten, we wouldn't be able to go visit Nana and Papa in Mexico for three months." My in-laws live in a tiny Mexican village on the Baja Peninsula, where we'd first experimented with extended travel.

She considered this for a moment before coming up with a solution. "Can we have a kitten when Nana and Papa are dead?" At that point, I realized I hadn't properly explained the dilemma.

"Okay, we have our kangaroo egg, and we've played on the playground. Are we ready to go?" I asked the family at large.

"I think so," said Mike.

"I'm tired," Emilia added.

"I have to poop," Ivy declared.

"Sure, honey," I said. "Let's go find a bathroom."

Of all that Australia has to offer, I have to say I was as impressed with the public bathrooms everywhere as I was with the diversity of wildlife and beautiful landscape. I took Ivy into the bathroom, and the other patrons were treated to Ivy's step-by-step narration of pooping. She's notorious for taking her time, which results in me having to spend a ridiculous amount of time in public restrooms. And it seems the smellier those restrooms are, the longer she takes, prompting me to repeatedly ask, "Are you finished?" "Are you done now?" "How about now?" And because I pepper her with these questions, she answers me with, "Not yet." "There's another one coming out." "It's coming out now." "I think there's another one." "No, wait. I'm done."

With the bikini shopping, dingo humping, and familiarization with the public restrooms, I felt we could call our Eumundi visit a success.

* * *

The next morning, we tackled homeschooling again in earnest. Five minutes in, I watched the physical manifestations of Emilia's mounting frustration. Her eyes teared, her face reddened, and she began muttering, "I can't do it. I can't do it." My previous tactics of calming her had failed, so I resolved that this time we would simply switch gears.

"Science time!" I declared.

"Are we going to do a project?" Ivy asked.

"Yes!"

"Are we going to do the kangaroo egg?" Emilia asked hopefully while still wiping at her eyes.

"Yes!" I wanted to do the kangaroo egg early enough in the trip so that the girls would forget about it by the time we returned to the States. I was mortified by the thought of their teachers finding out that I'd tried to pass off a "kangaroo egg" as an actual science experiment. And I was sure, at that moment, that science hated me.

"I'll get the bowl," Ivy said.

"I'll get the water," Emilia added.

This would unfortunately result in what appeared to be a preserved fetal kangaroo in our kitchen for the next week. Ostensibly a child's toy, the disturbing replica of a kangaroo emerging from an egg submerged in water was grosser than a real baby kangaroo making its way from its mother's birth canal up into the pouch, which is one of those amazing feats of nature where you find yourself rooting for what looks like a tiny bloody booger.

When we had the kangaroo well on its way to hatching, we took a break for lunch before I reintroduced Emilia to the assignment that had been the cause of her frustration earlier that day. She completed it without tears, and I felt a true sense of victory. We entered the afternoon finally having hit the trifecta of simultaneously completing homeschooling, remaining calm, and feeling happy.

"No!" Mike cried from the corner of the house that he'd set up as his office. The distress in his voice was considerable. I knew that it signified a technical malfunction, which causes him far more distress than physical injury. My calm, happy sense of victory was revoked.

"What happened?"

"My cocktail. A drop of water. Touch pad." In his shock, he struggled to communicate, but a drop of condensation from the bottom of his cocktail glass had fallen onto his computer, and apparently it only takes one drop to corrupt the functionality of a laptop mouse pad. Which is unfortunate, because nothing goes well with work as much as a good cocktail.

The importance of our laptops is crucial. A downed machine takes the digital out of digital nomad. And no matter how many contingency plans we come up with, from online backups to hard drive replicas, something will go wrong, as in the case of Mac versus gin and tonic.

We located a store in Mooloolaba called I Love Computers, which could also be named Bend Over Because We Know How Much You Depend On Your Computer. The part was cheap, the labor was not, and to expedite the job (which in truth took them about ten minutes), we forked out an additional hundred dollars.

When I thought of what our various workdays entailed, I decided that compared to a major computer malfunction, getting through a few homeschooling tears wasn't so bad. And when it comes to the latter of the two, a cocktail (for the adult, of course) will only make it better.

* * *

A Formal Apology

The country has less than 1 percent of the world's population but more than 20 percent of its slot machines.

—Bill Bryson, *In a Sunburned Country*

It's not that bad.

I sucked in my stomach and turned to the side, the act all women are familiar with and are compelled to do when surveying themselves in a mirror.

Really, it's not that bad.

I hadn't had a chance to see what I looked like in my new swimwear but had guessed I'd looked pretty good based on Mike's reaction. The trouble with this is that someone you have sex with on a regular basis is not always the best judge of these things.

It's really not that bad.

I turned to see my butt and immediately winced, but told myself again, *It's not that bad.*

And then I destroyed the shreds of hope to which I'd been clinging. I'm not sure why—perhaps the devil made me do it, maybe it was morbid curiosity—but while looking at my ass in a fairly skimpy bikini, I clenched my buttocks.

Oh my god that's horrible! No it's not. Body shame is bullshit. Body shame is bullshit!

"Mama, you look beautiful."

I yelped with the realization that I was not alone.

"I mean, thank you, Ivy," I said, wondering how long she'd been in the room. I followed this with a silent but formal apology to anyone headed to the beach that day who might be subjected to me in a bikini.

"What's that on your back?" she asked.

"Mommy's gunshot wound? Or the scar from the grizzly bear?" I asked. My dermatologist has cut a fair amount of flesh from my upper back to ward off potential skin cancers, and I don't tend to heal well. If I have to suffer through such things, and horrific scars as a result, I feel it's my right to come up with more adventurous origins for them.

"It looks like chicken."

"What? What do you mean?" I wasn't sure I liked that. Did my flesh remind her of the dimpled, pale atrocity that is raw chicken skin? Or did she envision the processed insides of a cooked nugget?

"What are you talking about?" Emilia asked as she joined us in the bathroom.

"Mommy's chicken," Ivy explained.

"Oh yeah, you mean the chicken on her back?" Emilia asked.

Ivy nodded.

"When did this chicken thing start?" I asked.

"Because it looks so yummy," Emilia said, a rationale I wasn't quite sure how to digest.

"Mom, what's your tattoo say?" Ivy asked.

"Literary." The word is tattooed across my lower back in giant letters, a nerdy version of the traditional tramp stamp.

"Because you like books?" Emilia asked.

"Yes."

"You must be really smart, Mom," Ivy said.

"Why, because I like books?"

"No, because you can read your tattoo without even looking at it."

I did my best to carry the children's compliments, that I was both yummy and really smart, with me to the beach that day. I fought the urge to spend the majority of the time sitting down in an effort to hide my butt from anyone's view and reminded myself that I feel no such judgment when seeing others in swimwear, and perhaps I would be well-served to be kinder to myself. That said, I certainly wouldn't be joining a game of beach volleyball. My most adventurous undertaking was a walk and exploration of the tiny creatures that inhabit the giant rock formations that separate two areas of beach. I did my best along this walk to try to feel comfortable in my bared skin, yet remain calm and avoid any unnecessary clenching.

* * *

On our final day in Queensland, I wanted to make sure we saw anything else on the Sunshine Coast that was worth seeing. The Australian Nougat Company was near Eumundi, Levi had mentioned it to us, and it was often billed on activity sites and guides as "world-famous." I had a hard time making sense of this, because nougat wasn't on my radar as something worthy of reaching fame. But there's a niche for everything, so I wasn't going to dismiss it just because I find

the word nougat distasteful. If you want to describe something that's supposed to be delicious, surely you can do better
than nougat. (I feel the same about anything that comes in
nugget form.) Australians don't pronounce the "t" at the end
of nougat, like Americans do, but that variation on pronunciation doesn't make the word any more palatable in my mind.
But since I kept hearing about the world-famous Australian
Nougat Company, I figured we'd better check it out.

As we drove toward the Nougat Company, I saw a sign
pointing us down a driveway.

"Is this it?" Mike asked as he pulled in toward a building
that appeared to be someone's home. The small parking lot
was empty.

"Hurry and park while there's still a space," I said. "I'm
sure the crowds will be pouring in any minute."

"Are we really going in there?" Mike asked.

"You bet your ass we are," I said. "How often does one get
to see nougat being made?"

"Are we at the candy factory?" Emilia asked.

"I bet they have chocolate and rainbow sprinkles!" Ivy
declared.

"You may have oversold the Nougat Company," Mike said.

"Or maybe it will be awesome," I countered.

We approached the two-story home to find that the Nougat
Company occupied the bottom floor, next to a garage bay. We
entered the small shop, approximately six feet by four feet. It
consisted of bars of nougat for sale, a wall of brochures advertising other attractions on the Sunshine Coast, a table with free
samples of nougat, and a television with two chairs in front
of it, on which one could watch a video of the nougat-mak-
ing process. This would have to suffice, as on the other side

of a glass wall—the actual factory part—no one was making nougat at the time.

On the video, nougat chefs mixed macadamia nuts, egg whites, sugar, and other ingredients and formed large slabs of nougat that were then cut into smaller bars. Also in the video, the chefs wore gloves when handling the nougat approximately 40 percent of the time. But I'm sure they washed their hands thoroughly. And when I say, "I'm sure," I mean "I really hope."

A woman appeared from behind a small counter and looked startled to see us.

"Hello," she said.

"Hello!" When I'm uncomfortable, I sometimes make up for it with inappropriate levels of enthusiasm.

She stared at me, expectantly.

"We're here to check out all the nougat!" I proclaimed.

"Well, there's the video of nougat being made."

"Yes, we saw that. It's lovely!"

"And if you like, you can take a picture with the first nougat paddle."

A large wooden paddle, resembling an oar, was mounted to a post.

"Awesome! Girls, come stand by the nougat paddle."

In just a few short years, I won't be able to get away with something like that. A request for my kids to stand by a large wooden paddle to have their picture taken will be met with rolled eyes, exaggerated shrugs, and heavy sighs. But luckily, we're not there yet. Emilia and Ivy hugged the paddle as if it was Mickey Mouse himself and smiled for the camera.

After that picture, there wasn't much left for us to do but buy some nougat. I selected four of the bars, despite the fact that after tasting a tiny rectangle from the free samples, I hadn't been tempted to return for seconds.

That night we met Levi and his family for a final, farewell dinner at the Buderim Tavern, which sits high in Buderim, almost as if perched on a cliff, with spectacular views of the land and beaches of the Sunshine Coast and Mooloolah Valley. It might seem odd to take children to a tavern, but in a stroke of genius, the establishment added a children's playroom, complete with a face-painting fairy. A bouncy house beckoned from the patio. They managed to find that perfect balance where you don't feel like you're eating in a kids' restaurant, which is my personal version of hell, but you also don't feel like you're taking your kids to a place that is inappropriate for them. It was a huge dining area, rather than a small, smoky bar, which is the image that comes to my mind when anyone says tavern. The children moved freely back and forth from our table to the playroom and remained in sight at all times and without bothering other patrons.

Many Australian restaurants operate on a different system of ordering, delivering, and paying for food than what we're used to in America. Levi walked us through the process, which began with ordering drinks in one area of the Tavern.

"If you want a beer," Levi advised, "make sure you ask for a *pint*."

"What do they normally give you?" Mike asked.

I wondered if Levi was saving us from unknowingly ordering a massive quantity of alcohol. I pictured restaurants in America where ordering a beer is followed by the question: "Sixteen- or twenty-four-ounce?" But Australia has thankfully not embraced the gluttonous inclinations that we're used to; no one was trying to push anything resembling a Big Gulp or

Super-Sized combo our way.

"If you don't order a pint, you get a ridiculous little glass of beer. Order a pint," Levi advised.

We did so before moving to a different counter where we placed our food order.

"What are pokies?" I asked Levi. A different wing of the Tavern advertised pokies, and I didn't know what that meant, but I'd seen signs prohibiting minors, which led my gutter-prone mind to all manner of activities in which poking could be used as the descriptive action. I'd seen signs for pokies often, but only with Levi did I have the courage to ask for clarification.

"Slot machines," he said sternly. "And I hate them. They're everywhere. You can go into a really nice bar or restaurant, but there will be these obnoxious slot machines that just ruin it. Gambling is definitely an issue in Australia."

When we were situated back at our table with respectable pints, awaiting the arrival of our food, Levi's wife nudged me. "Amanda, look who just walked in."

I'm not sure who I expected to see when I turned around. It would have to be a celebrity, because everyone I knew in Australia was sitting there at the table. I was hoping for Hugh Jackman but turned instead to see Santa Claus strolling into the Tavern, complete with a sack slung over his shoulder, heading straight for the playroom. The face-painting fairy came up for air as the children flocked from her to Santa. I wondered if my children would note Santa's Australian accent, but they were too eager to believe, and his presentation was too convincing, for variances in pronunciation to allow any doubt into their minds. Not only did Santa hand out toys to the children from his large sack of wonders, but they were *individually wrapped* gifts. Above and beyond what I would have expected. Emilia received a sparkle-filled ball that lit up when bounced, and Ivy got a pink journal.

Going out to a nice restaurant and finding entertainment for the kids in the form of a playroom is wonderful. Throw in a face painter, and you bring it up a notch. But then to have a fairly convincing Santa enter the picture and hand out wrapped gifts was exceptional. I kept waiting for Santa to slip me a bill, but he never did. I guess what made it even more special was that the Tavern didn't have any signs on display advertising Santa's visit. His appearance and doling out of gifts hadn't been heralded. It was just a perfect, unexpected bonus. And it worked in the Tavern's favor, of course, as the longer you keep the children happy, the more money their parents will spend.

"So we finally made it to the Nougat Company," I told Levi.

"The what?"

"The Nougat Company. The place you were telling us to go to."

"What the hell is nougat?"

This made no sense, given Levi's earlier endorsement of the place.

"Nougat. You know, the sweet stuff in a candy bar, only at the Nougat Company they make an entire bar that's just nougat. You told us to check it out, said it might be fun for the kids."

"*Ginger*," Levi clarified. "I told you to go to the *Ginger* Factory. There's a little train, and the gingerbread man goes all over the world. It's really awesome."

The Ginger Factory sounded really cool, but we were leaving the Sunshine Coast early the next morning and didn't have any more opportunities to visit local attractions, and we'd spent our last day taking pictures of a wooden paddle and sampling nougat in a variety of flavors, like white chocolate macadamia cranberry and macadamia ginger, which, let's be honest, were not fantastic no matter how many pretty words you put in front of nougat.

We said a bittersweet farewell to Levi and his family, trying but likely failing to express our gratitude for their help, generosity, and friendship. In addition to voicing these things, I wanted to give them a small token of appreciation. It was a bar of nougat.

* * *

The next morning, we woke early to finish packing and to clean the house. I wanted to make sure we left everything spotless and made a mental note to check for fingerprints on the naked bust that Ivy liked to fondle.

I washed all of the sheets and hung them out on the line to dry. I cleaned every inch of the white floor and glass windows. I was determined to positively represent people who travel with small children and prove that it need not imply dirt and damage. Everything was near perfect. Mike had the kids and all of our belongings packed in the rental car, when a loud clap of thunder shook the house.

"Amanda, let's go," he called. "I want to beat the rain."

I didn't understand this concept. How exactly can we beat the rain? What if the rain was headed in the very direction we would travel? And it's not as if we haven't driven in rain before or were contending with a leaky vehicle. But Mike was remembering earlier rains on the Sunshine Coast, rains of such magnitude that he referred to them as rivers in the air.

"I'm not ready," I called back.

"Let's go," he demanded.

I ran out to the laundry line. The sheets were almost dry, and I couldn't leave them there for the homeowner to find, soaking in the oncoming storm. I grabbed them from the line, raced back inside, and loosely draped them on each of the beds from which they'd been taken, then scribbled a hasty addendum to the long note I'd left for the Artiste, explaining where things were and why.

"What are you doing?" Mike asked when I got down to the car.

"You know, instead of yelling at me to hurry, you could always come help me finish," I said.

"I want to get out of here before the rain comes," he repeated.

This was a moment all married couples experience, when you realize that you are operating on two entirely different planes of logic. Sometimes the appropriate action is to further and fully explain your position to your spouse. More often it's best to move on, which is what we did.

We took the M1 south toward Brisbane. We would retrieve our new home in the form of a camper van. Then Mike would drive the camper, and I would follow in the rental car to return the car to its owners. After an hour's drive, we found the rental office where we'd retrieve our Britz campervan. A corner of the office held a small children's area, for which I was thankful. A man waited in line ahead of us, but no staff were present behind the counter. I had the impression this might take a while. I imagined the sound of crickets.

We waited for a good ten minutes, the man in front of us as befuddled and powerless as we were, with no clear plan other than to keep waiting.

"I'm going to call," Mike said. He retrieved his phone and dialed the number of the office in which we stood. We heard the muffled ring of a phone that was never answered. He hung up after fifteen rings.

"They're probably, you know, making our camper all spiffy," I ventured.

"They're probably out back smoking," Mike said.

"At least the kids are happy."

A minute later, and just short of the onset of a panic attack, two Britz staffers appeared. A young woman took charge of us, and we began the extensive paperwork process that accompanies renting a vehicle that will also serve as your home. We bought sanitizer packets for the camper toilet and declined the extra insurance needed if we rolled the vehicle entirely.

"I don't think we need that," Mike said.

"It really only happens if you're swerving to avoid a kangaroo or something like that," she said.

And I knew at that moment that if he found himself needing to swerve to avoid a kangaroo, my husband would likely mow the animal down instead, in fear of rolling the vehicle.

"Okay, you're all set then, returning the vehicle in Melbourne." She circled relevant dates and numbers for assistance in the mountain of paperwork and then slid it our way. "If you just want to wait in front of the building there, I'll pull the vehicle around."

We were then introduced to what would be our home for the next two weeks and approximately 2,000 kilometers (or 1,200 miles).

"Oh my lord," I said when she pulled the camper to a stop in front of us.

"Whoa," said Mike.

"It's huge." I'm not sure what I expected. I knew the vehicle would have a toilet, small kitchen, and two beds, but in my mind, all of the amenities were magically condensed into a vehicle the size of a regular van. And not a creepy, window-less, predator van but an endearing little Volkswagen sort. The behemoth in front of us reminded me more of a U-Haul suited for the transport of the furnishings of a five-bedroom home.

Emilia and Ivy remained inside the rental office, and I again marveled at the wisdom of occupying children at certain times. I'm not a fan of kids on "devices," but sometimes you just need a carpet square and a few brightly colored toys. The last thing we needed when learning how to operate the camper, which included five million buttons to be activated in a precise order, was being peppered with questions from the kids along the way.

We were shown how to operate the water heater, toilet, water tanks, electricity, stove, awning, and other amenities. My head hurt because I knew that I would remember no more than one-sixteenth of the instructions when we finally reached our spot for the night and attempted to set up camp. Mike is far more capable in such scenarios, and I trusted that he was taking it all in.

With the paperwork squared away and the tour complete, we moved all of our luggage from the car to the camper.

"There's a spot inside the office," the woman advised, "where people leave behind items they don't need anymore. You're welcome to have a look and take what you like."

"Do you want to go check it out?" Mike asked. "I can finish loading everything."

For some reason, when she'd mentioned it, I'd turned my nose up at the idea. Surely we didn't need anyone else's *leftovers*; we had a mountain of belongings as it was. But on Mike's suggestion, I decided to at least walk *by* the pile of other people's items that would be of no use to us.

Five minutes later, I emerged with more than I could carry. Because as much as I'd dismissed the free pile of stuff, thinking we had everything we needed, I only had to take one look at the paper towels, plastic wrap, and dish soap to know that I'd been severely mistaken. And the camper was costing us thousands of dollars, so I might as well offset a minuscule portion of the expense by saving on a few needed items we'd otherwise have to purchase. Once I accepted that I'd be pilfering another's discarded items, my snobbery went out the window, and before I knew it, I was contemplating partially used items, like cooking spray and olive oil, and even more intimate items, like half a sleeve of cookies and a quarter of a jar of Nutella. Thinking that someone could have stuck his finger in there and licked the Nutella off was gross. I took it anyway.

Mike drove the camper, and I followed in the rented car. Emilia and Ivy rode in the camper, because they were excited about this new vehicle of endless wonder and adventure. And also because Mike still felt better about having them in his care, which was fine by me. The camper was bigger and therefore seemed less likely to injure all of its inhabitants in the event of an accident or the dreaded fiery crash. And if the rental car, which I drove, did end up in a fiery crash, I agreed that I didn't want the kids in there with me. We caravanned back to the owners of the bearded dragon, which the girls once again doted on as we handed over the keys.

The official trading of our home and car for a caravan signified an abrupt end to our cushy accommodations. Luxury was gone. I'd been a fool to lament my lack of privacy while living in the home in Buderim, because that had been nothing compared to what we were in for.

* * *

Byron Bay

It is a miracle that curiosity survives formal education.

—Albert Einstein

The camper was cumbersome; it lumbered and swayed. Riding in it gave me the sense that it was too much of everything: too tall, too wide, too long, and too heavy. But with each minute of driving without a catastrophe, or even a minor incident, my sense of dread abated.

"Why can't we ride up there?" Emilia asked, pointing to the bunk above the vehicle's cab. She and Ivy were buckled into the passenger seats behind Mike and me, and their position seemed terribly unfair to them, given all of the far more interesting spaces that the camper had to offer.

At times, I will answer such questions with explanations of safety and how far an unrestrained body can travel in the event of a high-speed (or even low-speed) impact. At other times, like this one, I revert to the more definitive, "It's the *law.*" This ends the conversation because they then conclude on their own that if I were to let them break the rule, our family would have to move to prison.

"I'm not sure this is the way I want to go," Mike said. We were following our Australian-accented GPS to Byron Bay, but it was leading us through downtown Brisbane. It looked to be a lovely city, but we didn't necessarily want to get a look while driving for the first time in an unwieldy vehicle. The streets narrowed as the traffic thickened, and we chided ourselves for not charting a course that would skirt the city, a mistake we would repeat in both Sydney and Melbourne.

"Everything's going to be fine." I encouraged Mike for the forty minutes it took us to navigate big-city traffic in an oversized camper. "You're doing great. Keep left." But I didn't *believe* everything was going to be fine. With every block we traveled, I was secretly convinced we were about to demolish an adjacent vehicle, and I was amazed that it never happened.

One hundred and seventy-four kilometers later, we reached Byron Bay with relief and found the caravan park. Mike waited in the camper with the girls while I dashed into the office to check in. I approached a long counter, behind which sat a young woman ready to help me. Next to her, a middle-aged woman spoke on the phone. She was both smug and angry and obviously speaking to the representative of a troublesome group of prior tenants. On the other side of the counter, a man of about the same age leaned in, listening intently and expectantly.

"Well, I have pictures of the damage done, so those charges stand," she snapped. The man smirked in encouragement.

I wondered what sort of damage could be inflicted on a campsite. A map in front of me showed the layout of the campground, which included spots for tents and camper vans like ours, and a row of cabin-like structures. The damage in question had likely occurred in one of the latter. It was apparent that the middle-aged couple were the owners and operators of the caravan park, and the dispute was with a group of youngsters who had partied too hard and failed to clean up after their revelry. I would later learn that we were smack in the middle of Schoolies Week, when recent high school graduates celebrate the completion of their high school education with sex, alcohol, and a series of bad decisions.

The young woman checked me in, and we both tried to ignore the tension of the conversation beside us. I returned to the camper with a map of the grounds and information about the facilities, including a six-digit code to enter the bathrooms, which seemed like terrible overkill.

We followed the map to our site. All of the sites were close together with narrow lanes to pull mammoth campers like ours in and out. We scoped it out from a distance first, trying to figure the best way to pull the camper in and get situated without plowing over any unsuspecting campers in their tents. As we surveyed the spot, I stood next to the camper, and Mike sat in the driver's seat and spoke to me through the window. The man who'd been in the office pulled up in a glorified golf cart.

"Do you need some help?" he asked me.

"We're just figuring the best way to pull it in," I said, smiling my most angelic smile, trying to avoid the suspicion and disdain with which he approached campers.

"Well, you want to pull up on the side so you step out of the camper onto the concrete," he said.

"Oh, we don't park on the concrete?" I'd assumed the slab was there so that the camper would be on level ground.

"It's where you set up your table. That's what it's there for."

He wasn't unkind but still had an edge, and I wondered if this was his year-round state or a temporary one for Schoolies Week.

I relayed this information to Mike, who nodded but still hesitated before pulling in.

The owner looked at me, expectantly.

"This is our first day in this thing," I explained, motioning to our monstrosity.

"Does he want me to pull it in for him?" the owner asked.

While a small part of me wanted to say yes, I knew the only answer was "no, thank you." Mike is highly capable, and relinquishing the parking of the giant camper was a recipe for ego reduction.

"I think we'll be just fine," I said.

The owner said nothing more and sat in his golf cart, waiting. He was obviously not going to move on until we were situated, and he fully intended to add the pressure of a hostile audience to the situation. Mike pulled the camper down the narrow lane and into the spot without incident, and the gruff man finally motored away.

The campground was packed, and compared to most of the occupants, we felt elderly, though there were two other families nearby with children. Other than that, everyone was a recent high school graduate. Ibis and bush turkeys roamed silently through the grounds, which sat atop a small bluff overlooking the beach and the bay itself. Brilliant flowers in purple and orange flanked the area. While I wasn't used to a cramped notion of camping (in Idaho, we purposely camp with no other humans, structures, or roads in sight), the surroundings and adventure of a new experience were exciting.

Since it was our first night, it took some time setting up the camper. We made the beds, put out the awning, table, and chairs, and put the few groceries we'd purchased in cabinets and the small fridge. One bed occupied the rear of the camper, while the other was overtop the driving cab and required a ladder to reach. A sign advised that the upper bunk was not meant for children, lest they fall and injure themselves.

"Mom, can we sleep up there?" Ivy asked, motioning to the upper bunk.

"Yes, you can!" I answered, and convinced myself that the sign was intended for toddlers. There was no way Mike and I would be trekking up and down the ladder and sleeping under the tomb-like low overhead of the upper bunk. While we set up camp, the girls played with Peyton, a girl of about five years of age staying with her parents in a nearby tent.

"Come on, girls. Say goodbye to your friend," Mike instructed. We'd finished the hard work and were ready to venture into Byron Bay.

The camp was located on the edges of downtown, and Byron Bay proved to be highly walkable. We strolled through town, heading toward a place called the Railway Station, which we'd heard had consistently good live music and was friendly enough to take kids early in the evening.

When we approached, I had second thoughts. A man policed the entrance, ostensibly to keep out teenage drinkers.

"Is it okay to bring kids in here?" I asked.

"Yes," he answered. "But only until ten o'clock."

I looked past him and saw that in addition to beer drinkers and a live band, there were a few other families milling about. And the idea that Emilia and Ivy could stay up past ten o'clock was preposterous anyway. We entered and found that most people were more intent on socializing and drinking beer than listening to the band, which resulted in empty seats in the front row. I ordered beer for Mike and me, and french fries and lemonade for the kids.

"What's this?" Emilia asked as I handed her a cup.

"Lemonade."

"Ooh, lemonade," she said. And she and Ivy looked at each other with big smiles. She took a sip, and her face immediately contorted. "Ick! It's spicy!"

"It is?" I took a sip myself, fearing that they'd mistakenly been given an alcoholic concoction. What sort of mother accidentally serves her daughters lemon drops? Or Lynchburg lemonade? But the drink was only Sprite, which Australians call lemonade, and something I should have known by then. My girls view anything with carbonation as spicy, which is fine with me, as it has delayed the soda addiction that will surely someday hit.

The band played and was excellent, a strong-voiced woman leading in a mix of rock and soul and folk. No one danced in the small area between us and the band, so Emilia immediately declared it her stage and danced, all by herself, with gusto. After a few songs, adults began trickling into the dance area, but everyone gave Emilia a wide berth and allowed her center stage. Emilia's dancing can best be described as an awkward mix of ballet, Irish step dancing, and dramatic pauses where her face affects a look of intense pride and accomplishment. We encourage this as much as possible.

A song ended, and the crowd clapped. Emilia blushed as if the applause was for her and the band was merely an accessory. The lead singer spoke into the mic. "Little girl, come here. What's your name?"

She handed the mic to Emilia.

"Oh god," I said. Emilia has been known, when given a mic, to be reluctant to relinquish it.

"Emilia," Emilia boomed into the mic.

"Are you here on holiday?" Emilia had learned that when an Australian asked if she was on holiday, this meant what we would call a vacation, while Ivy, when posed the same question, always answered, "Christmas," thinking she'd been asked which was her *favorite* holiday.

"Yes," Emilia answered into the mic. "And do you know what?"

I groaned silently, worried that she'd broadcast something like "My mom has two chickens on her back." Inappropriate or random statements like that have been made to strangers before. And while I know it is in some way endearing, I still feel the occasional sense of dread when I don't know what my child is thinking and her voice is being amplified to dozens of people.

"What?" asked the bandleader.

"I'm from America."

"Oh really?" The singer feigned surprise, and the crowd laughed. "Well, would you like to help us out on our next song?"

Emilia was doing great, but I still held the same mix of pride and dread. Surely she wouldn't ask Emilia to sing along? As an accomplished musician who had clearly sung and played in front of many crowds before, she'd know better than to hand over the microphone to a seven-year-old kid, right? My worries dissipated as she handed my daughter a small egg shaker and told her to keep the beat. I love the egg shaker. It's an instrument not so loud as to drive you insane if your child has one at home and runs around the house with it. It also wouldn't be loud enough to actually disrupt the band if Emilia lost the beat, which she did a minute later. Mostly, I like the egg shaker because it is one of the few instruments that I can play without feeling musically inept. This is because I am musically inept.

We stayed for a few more songs, and Emilia danced, taking her shaker very seriously along the way. When I told her it was time to go, she approached the lead singer in between songs and attempted to return the shaker.

"You can keep that," the singer said. "That's a little gift from me to you, a souvenir from Byron Bay."

"Thank you," Emilia said. "But hold on just a second." She dashed to our table, grabbed Ivy by the hand, dragged her up to the stage, and presented her to the lead singer. "This is my sister, Ivy." She didn't need to say more. The message was clear: *while I'm very grateful, what do you have for my sister?*

"Oh, right," said the singer, and she graciously produced a second egg shaker and gave it to Ivy.

* * *

The next morning began with the irrefutable statement, "I need to go potty." I took the girls to the camp facilities in order to minimize the number of times I'd have to empty the camper toilet, a job that was mine and one to which I did not look forward. I was glad we had our own toilet, of course, because a middle-of-the-night pee is made worse when you have to trek through the dark past campers to a public facility, but in the daytime, we'd use the camp facilities whenever possible. The bathrooms were surprisingly and impeccably clean. I'd expected that camp restrooms would be on par with those at a truck stop. After we'd used the facilities and brushed teeth and hair, the girls played with Peyton and stalked ibis around the campsite while Mike and I logged in a few digital hours on our laptops. The free Wi-Fi of the campsite came with unexpected limitations on usage. For Mike, this was an annoyance, as the Internet is key to his productivity. He would supplement the camp connection with his backup plan of a portable connection. It was expensive to use but not nearly as financially devastating as if he'd been unable to work at all. I enjoyed the digital limitations and reserved my Internet usage for nonnegotiable tasks, like bill paying, and shed myself of social media updating, which was entirely liberating.

After the equivalent of a full workday and ten pathetic minutes failing at homeschooling, we readied ourselves to turn off the computers and venture out. I called the girls, and they came running, Peyton trailing behind.

"Can Peyton come with us?" Ivy asked.

"No, Peyton has to stay with her family." Peyton looked like a little firecracker of a girl, her spark temporarily snuffed on hearing the news that we weren't going to let her join us, but I hadn't even met her parents and kidnapping wasn't on my list of things to do.

Instead of heading into downtown as we had the day before, we walked through the campground to where it bordered a beach, then along the beach in the general direction of town. After a short walk, we crested a hill that opened up to a larger stretch of beach where hundreds of people gathered. We investigated and found that this was a competition of the Nippers. This is the kids' version of Surf Life Saving Australia. When you have a country with this many beautiful beaches, where the landscape of the coast beckons even the most timid of people to frolic in the water, you need to take lifeguarding to a new level, which is what happened in Australia. Kids who join the Nippers learn water safety and competency, like the Girl Scouts or Boy Scouts, only the marine version. We watched the competition during which nine-year-old girls grabbed kneeboards, raced into the sea, and paddled out to buoys in a fierce relay. Some of them couldn't make it out, and the breaking waves swept them half a mile down shore, at which point they would exit the water, carry their boards back to the starting point, and try again. Not once did I see a child exit the water in tears and frustration.

"Damn," said Mike.

"Yeah," I agreed. "Australian kids are badass."

Later in the day, we returned to the section of beach closer to the campsite and settled in near a large rocky area.

"Mom, will you play with me in the water?" Ivy asked.

"Sure," I said.

Ivy's water skills are on par with mine. Which is to say, she doesn't have any. Emilia had learned at least how to survive in a pool without a floatation device, and she loved to boogie board in the ocean. But Ivy was still in the age of "floaties" and furiously wiping her eyes any time water got near them. If we'd lived in Australia, perhaps she would have been a Nipper and overcome her tentativeness. Or, she would be the one kid exiting the water in tears and frustration after being swept down the beach.

We stood in water that reached only our shins, and I lifted Ivy every time the remnants of a bigger wave rolled in upon us. It was the same activity you usually see a parent engaged in with their baby, but I was still stuck in that phase with my five-year-old. When your kid weighs forty pounds, you can only play that game for so long, so we turned our attention to forming an ocean habitat inside a bucket. We filled it with sand and water and collected tiny clams, crabs, snails, and a baby jellyfish. We observed them in the world we'd created for them before returning them all to the sea and heading back to camp. The memory of failed homeschooling that morning dissipated, because unlike the grotesque kangaroo hatching, creating a miniature habitat and observing a variety of sea creatures truly would count as an enriching, hands-on, and enjoyable science experiment. And for a brief time, Ivy and Emilia convinced themselves that they had pets.

* * *

"Mom, can we have dinner?" Emilia asked.

"Sure," I said, "Ramen noodles it is!"

"Can Peyton have dinner with us?" Ivy asked.

Peyton stood behind Ivy, looking wide-eyed, hopeful, and grubby.

"Peyton, if you go ask your parents, then it's okay with me."

She dashed in the direction of her tent. A moment later, a slight woman emerged and gave me a wave of assent.

I set the three girls up at the outside camp table, and they devoured the Ramen, a few crackers, and some apple slices, as if it was fine dining.

We'd had so much fun at the Railway Station the night before that we decided to head back. As we closed up camp and prepared to head into town, Peyton's mother approached.

"Hi," I said. I saw now that she wasn't simply slight but frighteningly thin.

"Are you heading into town?" she asked. Apparently, we were skipping introductions.

"Yes."

"So are we," she said. "Peyton wants to go with you."

It took me a moment to realize what she was saying. I wasn't sure how to respond. After all, she hadn't asked me a question. She was simply stating that Peyton wanted us to adopt her, and I could tell that Peyton's mom hoped I would offer to take Peyton with us, despite the fact that we didn't know anything about one another. I didn't even know her name.

Mike must have overheard and probably feared that I'd offer to take Peyton, because he quickly materialized by my side.

"Well, we don't even know where we're going or what time we'll be back," he said. That was half-true.

To counter Mike's presence, Peyton showed up by her mother's side.

"I want to go with them, Mom."

"Yeah, that's not going to work," I said.

"You're going to have to go with us," her mother said. And both mother and child looked disappointed that we weren't amenable to the situation. They turned, dejected, and walked back to their camp. I caught a glimpse of Peyton's dad, who also looked frighteningly thin, which pretty much ruled out anorexia on the part of the mom. For a moment I wondered if they were homeless, but the caravan park wasn't cheap, which led me to the likelihood of significant drug use going on in Peyton's family.

The next morning, Peyton's family was gone. Emilia and Ivy lamented the loss of their friend, but Mike and I breathed a sigh of relief. In the little girl's absence, our daughters sought out the other family nearby with children. There seemed to be a *lot* of children, ranging from toddler to teenager. When we finally made all of our introductions, we learned they had six children, with names like Snow Poppy and Island Bleu. Initially, I was tempted to roll my eyes at such monikers, fearing that people who gave their children such names would also pressure me into participating in a drum circle or want to have a long discussion about my troubled aura. But that judgment was in error. We would come to know them as the kindest, most inherently good people we'd ever met. Their teenage girl would spend hours with Emilia, holding her hands as Emilia rolled along the sidewalk on their skateboard. Everyone in their family seemed incredibly talented too. Their nine-year-old boy busked on the street and sang us a song he'd written himself. It was eloquent, mature beyond his years. And his voice and his guitar skills were impressive.

As soon as he'd finished, Emilia said, "I can sing too," and launched into an a cappella version of *Frozen's* "Let It Go." The family of eight sat patiently and politely as Emilia sang. When she finished, they clapped, at which point she leapt into another song from the *Frozen* soundtrack and couldn't understand why I interrupted and wouldn't let her continue.

This family was not the nicest, most talented family we'd meet in Australia; they were the nicest, most talented family we've met in the world. Over the next day, Emilia would insert herself into their lives as much as she could. They always welcomed her, and I knew that if she was out of sight, she'd made her way to their camp.

When I'd retrieve her, apologetic for the intrusion, to which they always replied that they were happy to have her, I'd often have wine in hand, and I couldn't help but wonder if to them, I was as Peyton's mother had been to me.

After three nights in Byron Bay, it was time to move on. I adored the camping experience, though all of our discipline with homeschooling and routine was gone. I reminded myself that the experiences our girls were having far outweighed the importance of completing worksheets. They hadn't completed any assignments, but that was okay. Singing, dancing, playing, learning about the Nippers, and naming clams the size of their pinkie fingernails had their own merits.

* * *

The Sex Lives of Koalas

The closest relative of the koala is the wombat.
They both have pouches which open towards the rear.
This is fine for the wombat, but koalas need strong muscles
ringing the pouch to keep the young one from falling out.

– Koalaexpress.com.au

Packing up to leave Byron Bay included the distasteful task of emptying out the camper toilet. The dump station for this was, in my mind, located in a spot to give the full camp a perfect view. Disposing of our waste in so public a place felt like pooping in front of strangers, so I went about the task early, before most of our neighbors had risen.

The process involved removing the holding tank, which moved on wheels with a long handle that popped out, much like a roller suitcase. The sound of the wheels on pavement resonated throughout the campground and seemed to compromise what I'd hoped to be a covert undertaking. I reached the dump site, lifted the lid, unscrewed the cap of our tank, and emptied it into the larger underground tank without a hitch. Maybe I'd been afraid of appearing as if I didn't know what I was doing, but really, there is only one way to pour crap down a drain. Or perhaps I'd feared getting splashed with human waste. In any case, the task was distasteful but manageable. I rinsed the tank using a hose provided, returned to the camper, and felt like I'd just accomplished something truly great.

We packed up the camper, secured the interior contents, and said our goodbyes to new friends. Readying ourselves to depart made me realize how much we'd come to adore Byron Bay in such a short time. It was beautiful, but so were the other towns we'd visited, for which I didn't feel the same affection. Were the beaches more pristine and the downtown more endearing? Was it the youthful vibe of carefree schoolies? The abundance of hippies and buskers? I didn't think so. The difference was the level of interaction we had in Byron Bay. With the exception of Levi and his family, we had little contact with others in Buderim; in hindsight, I saw a certain level of voluntary isolation. In Byron Bay, in a campsite where your neighbors are a few feet away whether you like it or not, interaction was unavoidable. All of those interactions, both good and bad, made the experience richer. Those connections are the reward for leaving behind routine and moving forward without knowing what is to come. For me, that's the heart of vagabonding.

As we began the six-hour journey south, I felt we'd mastered the camper after just three nights and was pleased with how smooth the process had been. These were the thoughts in my head as Mike pulled onto the highway and picked up speed. Thoughts that were interrupted by a sharp crack as the ladder used to get to the top bunk flew from the narrow spot where it was stored, not having been securely stowed. Drawers crashed open, as we'd failed to lock them. I scurried about, trying to fix all of the things we'd neglected to do. A toilet reek filled the camper, but I didn't know what to do about that. Maybe we hadn't mastered anything.

The drive south took us past the Banana Coast and the Gold Coast. Having also spent a month on the Sunshine Coast, I wondered if, for something to truly be named a Coast in Australia, it had to be preceded by a yellow element.

Warnings of watching speed cameras speckled the highway. These signs were complemented with billboards assuring you that if you did speed, you would die and/or kill someone else. I became fascinated by these billboards and looked forward to reading each new one as we approached. From a distance, I spied one that depicted a man with a look on his face of severe constipation. I wondered what could cause him such distress. Had he sped and killed someone? Or was he just wrestling with the discomfort of his immovable bowels? We got closer, and the accompanying text read: Jesus is the answer.

Along the drive, we saw giant replicas of products, so that highway travelers could easily identify a business's wares. A golf ball seven feet in diameter, a shrimp the size of a house, a giant banana, a monstrous beehive, which seemed even more so when I contemplated the size of a bee that would inhabit such quarters.

The girls snacked on fruit and granola bars along the way, which Ivy described as "good delicious." She also liked to use the term "correct right." Brevity of language has never been her strong suit.

"Mom, I need to tell you something," she said.

"Okay."

"Well, actually, I need to tell you two things."

"Go ahead, Ivy. Just say what you need to say."

"The first thing I need to tell you is that even though my granola bar was good delicious, I'm still hungry."

"Okay."

"And the second thing I need to tell you is that I forgot what the second thing is."

After six hours of such exchanges, we reached Port Macquarie and located a caravan park. It was immediately apparent how different caravan parks can be. While the previous park had pavement and was structured and ordered, almost grid-like, this one had towering trees, huge expanses of grass, and plenty of space in between sites. We checked in and pulled into our spot. Mike and Emilia began setting everything up while Ivy and I walked over to the bathroom. As triumphant as I felt emptying the toilet tank that morning, it was a job I wanted to do as few times as possible. Along the walk to the facilities, we passed by a few structures that could be described as either cabin or trailer, and both would be correct (right). Some of these were short-term rentals, while others were home to permanent residents of the park. Outside of one, a woman used large shears to prune a tree.

She smiled and said g'day as we passed. Ivy commented, "Mom, that woman had really big scissors."

"Yes, she did. Those are called pruning shears."

"I sure hope she doesn't cut her leg off."

We made it to the bathroom and back without witnessing any impromptu amputations. Once we had camp set up, we set about Mike's first priority, scoping out the beach. It was a short walk from the caravan park to Shelley Beach, the southernmost of Port Macquarie's six main beaches and a less crowded alternative to Port Macquarie's more popular Flynn's Beach, which boasts restrooms and a surf club.

"Let's make a habitat!" I suggested. Creating a miniature sea world in a bucket had become my new favorite beach activity. I adored the tiny clams and crabs and snails, it allowed me to linger near the water's edge and avoid forced ocean frolicking, and the hands-on experience assuaged the guilt that accompanied my growing acceptance of the fact that life in a camper van was putting a startling halt on our academic progress.

"Mom, I found something new," Emilia called. She brought me something I'd never seen before. "What is it?"

"I don't know," I said. "Maybe part of a shell necklace?" Hundreds of tiny shell fragments were strung together. They were minuscule, and the work would have been both maddening and meticulous. "No, I don't think this could be man-made."

"Can I keep it?" she asked.

"I don't know, Emilia. It's so . . . pliable. I think it's an actual creature. I think we should return it to the sea."

"Hey, I found one too," Ivy said, and approached me with a similar curiosity, though Ivy's find was on the beach and had dried, losing much of the elasticity that the first one retained. I would later research the oddity and find that it wasn't a living creature but had been home to one. The pliability was due to the fact that what appeared to be a string was actually a tube, which served as the outer habitat of the plume worm, the creature that would have lived inside at one point, collecting the various shell fragments in an odd form of home décor.

The main attraction of Port Macquarie, in my mind, was not the beach but the koala hospital, and once I'd learned that such a thing existed, I was determined to go there. The hospital nurses its patients but also allows the public to access and tour the facility, which raises money to keep the operation going. The intensive care unit of the hospital is restricted to staff, but koalas who are close to being released or who are permanent residents of the hospital occupy quarters where the public can observe them.

"Does anyone know," asked the tour guide, "what the number-one ailment of our patients is? Why do you think most koalas end up in the koala hospital?"

The two guesses that came to my mind were animals injured by vehicles or bush fires. And both calamities had brought koalas to the hospital, but not nearly on such a scale as chlamydia.

"Mom, what's chlamydia?" Emilia asked loudly. The tourists and staff around us snickered.

"It's something that makes you sick," I whispered.

"Can people get it?"

"Yes."

As sure as I knew my child, I knew what she would say next. The same thing she says when learning of any ailment or tragedy that can befall a human. And she broadcast it loudly.

"I sure hope I don't get chlamydia."

"Me too, sweetie. Me too."

The sex lives of koalas are far more dramatic than one might initially think. The animal is threatened not only by STDs like chlamydia, which can prove fatal if not treated with antibiotics, but also a form of HIV. If you were a female koala who managed to stay disease-free, you would still have to deal with aggressive male koalas who might physically rip you down from a eucalyptus tree to have their way with you at any moment. And while the male koala makes a deep grunting sound you'd expect from an elephant or large pig, the female has an eerie scream. If yanked from a tree, she's apt to scream and fight off her would-be mate. These screams attract other males, who then duke it out for the spoils, while the female hangs back to try to figure out which one is the dominant male and future baby daddy.

Koalas were often called koala "bears" because they resembled teddy bears, but the more I learned about these creatures (through my own research—koala hospitals and rehabilitation centers don't give all the gory details, though they did cop to chlamydia), the more it became apparent that comparing them to sweet and cuddly objects of comfort is nothing more than wishful thinking on the part of humans. Take motherhood, for example. Not only does the joey cling to the female koala's teat, but at six months, the joey also begins to eat a fecal pap that the mother produces. In essence, mom must lactate *and* poop special food. Motherhood is demanding enough as it is. Having to provide food for your child from more than one orifice is downright cruel.

All mothers know that giving birth severely compromises our bladder control ever after. That's why we women who have given birth try to quickly cross our legs before we sneeze. But on top of that, koalas have a rear-facing pouch, so designed by Mother Nature so that the joey can reach the aforementioned fecal pap. If the mother is upright, gravity therefore endangers the joey of falling out, requiring the mother koala to have an additional sphincter in the form of a ring of muscles around the opening of the pouch. She must be able to clench that sucker shut to protect her young. I'm not denying that baby koalas are cute. Baby *anythings* are cute. But come on. An added sphincter? The care and protection of these babies seems terribly taxing on the mother. Then again, she doesn't have a minimum of eighteen years of said taxation.

We returned to the camper where I tried to blot the words fecal pap from my mind. Mike suggested we empty the camper's gray water for the first time. This is the tank with water that's been run through the sink or shower, the latter of which we hadn't yet used, thus far opting for the camp facilities. We had used the sink a fair amount in the course of brushing teeth and cooking meals.

Most campsites had a specific area for dumping gray water. I went to the office to inquire where this was, as I couldn't find it.

"You can just let the gray water out on the grass," the man said. "Yeah, it's got lots of good stuff in it; it's good for the grass."

"Okay," I answered. This was in stark contrast to every other campsite we would encounter, where dumping your gray water on the grass was strictly prohibited, and I decided that whether or not there was "good stuff" in the gray water would depend heavily on what it had been used for before entering the "gray" classification.

"Let's see," said Mike. "There's this hose here that we attach to the pipe that releases the gray water." He wrestled with attaching the hose, which was a good indication that it wasn't going to attach at all. On the whole, my husband is competent with such things. "But it looks like the connection is broken, so . . ." The gray water began to dribble out messily.

"Oh dear lord," I pulled up the neckline of my T-shirt to cover my nose and mouth. I hadn't thought emptying the gray water would be a big deal. After all, it was just the water from washing hands and dishes, and surely the task couldn't compare to emptying the toilet. But I was mistaken. This wasn't just soapy water; it included bits of food. It was where we brushed our teeth. The combination was putrid. The stench was nauseating, and I made a mental note not to purchase any more cans of tuna.

When the gray water tank was fully drained, we scrubbed our hands and arms as if trying to ward off ghastly contaminants. Ironically, this act only created more gray water. Like the toilet tank, it was simply a reality of living in a camper, so I decided I might as well surrender to it and take advantage of the amenities it held. That night I would use the shower in the camper. We'd paid for such perks; we might as well make use of them.

The shower and toilet occupied the same small cubby, and when I opened the door, I saw with dismay that there was a leak. Intermittent rain throughout the day had seeped in, and while it might not seem problematic to have a leak in a place where one will shower anyway, this was also the site of the toilet. I was confronted with the depressing sight of a wet roll of toilet paper, which I have never found to be at all redeemable.

I had my soap and shampoo at the ready. The water heater was on. I waited for a ridiculous length of time for the water to warm, but it never did.

"How's it going in there?" Mike called.

"I'm waiting for hot water," I yelled.

"Just shower," he advised. "You're filling our gray water tank back up."

"Hot water, my ass," I muttered, and took the most uncomfortably invigorating (but also the quickest) shower of my life.

Between the ill-fitting gray water hose, leaking bathroom, malfunctioning water heater, and a variety of unpleasant odors, our camper was suddenly less endearing to me than it had been just twenty-four hours prior.

That night, we dined on our staple of peanut butter and jelly. Reincorporating foods like PB and J and Ramen noodles made me feel eighteen again, when a lack of finances and cooking know-how made cheap foods the norm. In that way, I could begin to see that travel keeps you young, because being young is largely about managing various states of discomfort, all in pursuit of an adulthood that's relatively comfortable. The problem with adulthood, of course, is that perpetual comfort can make you stagnant and soft.

When we were young and just starting out as a couple, we lived in various shoebox apartments, where toilets needed plunging, appliances rarely worked, and most problems were met with the temporary fix of duct tape. At one point, we lived on a leaky, rented, thirty-foot boat in California. But when you are young, you approach the discomfort as a series of challenges to survive and to which you can adapt, rather than things that need to be escaped. When you are young, you don't need to get out of your comfort zone, because you haven't yet found your comfort zone. I could see the benefit in any hardships we'd ever had, the growth that emerged as a result, and an affirmation of how important travel and occasional uncertainty are. They combat the staleness of comfort and routine and keep youthfulness alive. I looked around at our living space within the confines of the camper, wondered how many days I had until I'd again have to empty the toilet tank, and felt very young indeed.

* * *

Clean Is the New Black

Step 1: Milking The Venom. The first step is getting your hands on a lot of snakes, which are quarantined and monitored for weeks to months to ensure their good health. Before milking, put on protective gloves.

– *Popular Mechanics*, "How to Make Antivenom—and
Why the World Is Running Short."

After six days in the camper, I began dreaming of the comforts of a crappy hotel room. The carpet would be worn, the bedspread frayed thin, and a lingering funk of urine and body odor would fill the air and later cling to our clothes. And yet, it would be glorious.

The drive to Port Stephens was long, but upon reaching our latest destination in New South Wales, we had to continue on a road that snaked out to Fingal Bay. For some reason, we'd reserved a campsite in the easternmost part of Port Stephens, on the Tomaree Peninsula. As we inched toward our caravan park, I could picture it on the map. I knew exactly why we'd chosen it. *Because* it was so far away, and because sometimes those destinations are the most intriguing ones. But as the camper crept farther out onto the peninsula, and the children groaned ever louder with that deadly combination of impatience and boredom, I doubted my earlier rationale while planning the itinerary.

The skies drizzled on us periodically in Port Macquarie, but the campsite had been protected by a canopy of towering eucalyptus. As we neared Fingal Bay, the drizzle that followed us matured into a rain that poured with purpose, the type of rain that brings to mind greater catastrophes than a leaky bathroom. Mike slowed to a crawl, and we pulled into our campsite, which offered no protection from the elements.

After thirty minutes of growing depression, parked in our campsite but unable to exit, hunkered down and fever-ishly dormant, the rain suddenly stopped. We emerged with the same caution as did the dozens of rabbits who called the caravan park home.

"It's not so bad when it's not raining," I said.

"Yeah, but I don't know how long it will last." Mike looked at the sky warily. "We should go to the store now so we can hurry back before it starts raining again."

"I don't want to go to the store," Emilia said. "Is that all there is to do in Australia? Go to the store?"

There have been instances like this in which my first reac-tion is to call my child an ungrateful little shit. Studies show that calling your child an ungrateful little shit, however, does not inspire in them feelings of gratitude, so I fell back on my go-to parenting tool: sarcasm.

"Yes," I answered. "If only we could have done something fun these past few weeks, like feed kangaroos or go to the beach or live in a camper van or meet Santa Claus in a bar. Oh, wait! We *have* done those things!"

"You're right," Emilia said with a bashful smile. "I'm just tired."

I wanted nothing more at that moment than to hug my daughter. She could have stayed in a funk, persisted in whining herself into a full meltdown, but instead she showed maturity, objective thinking, and a willingness to change her mind. With pride, I took her hand, and we walked behind Ivy and Mike.

"Do they have snacks at the store?" Ivy asked.

"They sure do," Mike promised.

By the time we returned from the store with snacks aplenty, the rain had resumed, confining us inside the camper. The girls napped intermittently and looked at books; Mike worked on his laptop. When we checked in, I'd picked up brochures of local attractions, as I always do, and I turned my attention to these. Apparently there were sand dunes nearby, which were fun to slide down. A brochure depicted gleeful families coasting down the dunes as if enjoying a ride at an amusement park. In the rain, of course, this would be a miserable experience. But the more I tried to picture the activity, the more I decided it was a terrible idea in perfect weather as well. Sand is a nemesis with the power to work its way into every crevice of my body when merely walking on it. The idea of inviting further intrusion by sliding down a dune on my ass was ludicrous.

It was a moot point though, because the rain refused to relent. Our location felt remote because of the taxing drive to get there, and now the oppressive weather intensified that feeling. We no longer felt we were in Australia. We didn't feel anywhere but trapped in our vehicle, inching ever closer to a state of mild insanity.

Twenty-four hours of rain later, Mike looked up from his laptop and said, "Maybe we should move on." We'd only stayed one night. Since we'd paid for two, it hadn't occurred to me that we could just leave. I'm never one to stray from a plan. The idea of changing a plan, even for a good reason, quickens my pulse and causes me palpable distress. I'm well aware of the fact that this makes me a fairly annoying person; that doesn't mean I can do much to change it. And this is why the concept of vagabonding, of nomadic undertakings without all of the pieces of the puzzle in place, is an exercise that's good for me.

"But where would we go?"

"To the next campsite," he said.

"But we don't have a reservation there until tomorrow."

"Maybe they can get us in a day early."

"But maybe they can't! That's why we made all of these reservations, because so many places were booked!"

"Amanda, we're living in a camper. We can always just park somewhere. Do you really want to spend another day in here while it pours outside?"

I had to agree. The rain showed no signs of abatement, and no amount of cute and fuzzy bunnies could offset the gloom of hunkering down in stormy weather.

"Okay," I relented, "but on the way out, let's stop at a grocery store."

"We just went to the store yesterday. What do we need at the store?"

"I want to get a big jug of water."

"Why?"

"*Why?*"

Mike was content filling our water bottles from questionable sources, whereas I view water as essential to survival and prefer to always have water on hand that I know is intended for drinking. We differ on this point, but I wasn't going to budge.

We drove to a Woolworth's, also known as Woolies, and Mike and Ivy stayed in the camper while Emilia and I dashed inside. At the checkout line, Emilia asked the clerk, "What's your name?"

"Steve." He smiled.

"I'm Emilia, and do you know what?"

"What's that?"

"I'm from America."

Steve feigned surprise, then gave Emilia a serious look and confided, "You know, I actually already knew that."

"You did?"

"Yes. Do you know how I knew?"

"Because I talk different?"

"That's right," he confirmed. "Emilia, would you like some Super Animal cards?"

"Yeah!" she cheered. "Thank you."

For every twenty dollars spent at a Woolworth's, a common grocery chain throughout Australia, we received a four-pack of Super Animals, trading cards with pictures of unique animals and facts about them. The girls loved them. In truth, I loved them too.

"Mom, what's saliva?" she asked as we walked back to the camper.

"Spit. Why?"

"Because . . ." she shuffled through her animal cards, "the Edible-Nest Swiftlet makes its nest out of its own solidified saliva."

"I'm not sure how I feel about that," I answered honestly.

"And the Bornean Slow Loris protects its babies by covering them in their toxic saliva before heading off to hunt."

"Well, you do have quite the salivary theme going on there, don't you?"

"What?"

"Nothing, sweetie. Nature is glorious."

We returned to the camper and readied ourselves for the next long drive, which meant making sure the girls had pillows and books at hand, and ensuring snacks and drinkable water were nearby for everyone.

"Are we ready to go?" asked Mike.

"Wait. I'm tired of things flying all over the place every time we drive. I want to make sure everything is locked and in place." The ladder was secure, the cabinets were locked, and I was sure that this time we could avoid the catastrophe that seemed to occur every time we put the camper in motion. "Okay, I think we're ready."

The camper lumbered to life, and as Mike took his first sharp turn, the three-gallon jug of water, which I'd assumed was heavy enough to stay put where I'd stowed it on the counter, slid off and landed on the floor.

"Mom, there's water!" Ivy yelled.

The jug had burst open on one side, and water poured across the floor, flowing into the well of the step, where all of our shoes were stored.

"Damn it!" I jumped out of my seat, picked up the jug, and tried to assess where the leak was, pouring water on my torso in the process.

"Everything okay back there?" Mike called from the driver's seat.

"No." I left it at that, biting my tongue to keep from further swearing in front of my kids. After I looked ready to compete in a wet T-shirt contest, I identified the location of the compromise in the jug, put it upside down to stop the water's escape, and placed it in the sink. Half of my precious water was gone, on my person and thoroughly soaking our shoes, but half remained and was in no danger of again flying through the air. I try not to be a glass-is-half-empty type of person, so I focused on the fact that the jug was half-full.

We continued south, and at one point it occurred to me that I didn't know the day of the week or the time of the day, which was both unsettling and liberating. Along with homeschooling, concern about my appearance had also gone by the wayside. I abandoned any attempts at makeup or jewelry. My only goal was to keep myself basically clean, and I decided that going beyond that was highly overrated. I strove simply not to smell bad. Clean was the new black.

We drove past countless places where I would have liked to stop, but once we were going in the camper, I was more inclined to just get to our next destination. Stopping and starting in the camper was a process that always seemed more complex than just pulling the car over to hop out for a quick look. Even if we had been in a car, it probably wouldn't have been a good idea to stop in at all of the breweries and wineries that caught my eye. But we also passed by signs for avocados, figs, and strawberries, all of which sounded wonderful.

We outdrove the rain, and I silently observed a large field dotted with lazy kangaroos. I knew that the kids wouldn't be able to see from their seats, and telling them that there were kangaroos that they couldn't see would surely lead to tears. I thought about covertly conveying the information to Mike but figured it best for him not to be distracted while navigating our monstrous, temporary home.

"Okay, now stick your tongue out," Emilia said.

"Okay," Ivy replied.

This was followed by copious giggling.

"Okay, now you stick your tongue out, and I'll touch it," Ivy said.

"I think our girls are making out in the backseat again," I said to Mike.

To someone without children, or even a parent of boys, this may seem like concerning behavior, but truly it's not. As long as they weren't subjecting others to their tongue-touching experimentation, I knew it didn't merit a reprimand.

"Hey, Mom, is that the big red rock?" Emilia asked.

She posed this question for any hill she saw while we were in Australia. She wouldn't have known about Uluru but for the librarian at her school in the States who, when learning Emilia would travel to Australia, told her about the rock and asked Emilia to bring back a picture. While I'm sure the sandstone rock formation is impressive, and perhaps one day I will see it, a two-day drive through barren land was not in the cards during this trip. I contemplated lying to Emilia, but if I told her the hill she saw was Uluru, she would want to stop the camper and take a picture for the librarian.

"No, Emilia. Like I said before, we're not going to get to see the big red rock on this trip." Even Australians had told us not to do so, lamenting the monotonous drive inland. And while flights were available, I couldn't stomach any more money on airfare than what we'd already spent getting to the land down under. "We'll buy a postcard of Uluru, but you're going to have to settle for that."

We'd driven for almost two hours when Mike suggested we stop. He took the exit for Gosford. I saw a sign for a reptile park but didn't mention it. We'd agreed we couldn't afford to keep spending money on zoos and aquariums, which, while always impressive, weren't cheap. But Mike seemed to be following the signs for the Australian Reptile Park in Somersby.

"Where are you going?" I asked.

"To the Australian Reptile Park," he said. He pulled into their parking lot, shut off the ignition, turned to me, and added, "They have wombats."

I knew then that this splurge was as much for me as it was for the children, because I had a burning, borderline obsessive desire to see a wombat.

We entered the park, and the girls were immediately drawn to the giant plastic replicas of crocodiles and tarantulas while Mike and I gravitated more toward observing the real creatures. We peered into a glass-walled room and watched as a woman extracted venom from large arachnids. She prodded the creatures gently with a stick, and when they attacked the stick, she used a long dropper to suck up the venom they dispensed.

The Australian Reptile Park has a long history of leading Australia in the research and production of antivenin. (Or antivenene or antivenom, as is commonly used these days. In my research into which is the correct term, I found that either works, though the debate can be as passionate and divisive among herpetologists and arachnologists as a political debate is to the general public.) In any case, I read with interest the history of the park and its founder, Eric Worrell, from the backyard zoo he kept as a boy (admission was a penny, and the attractions included snakes, frogs, guinea pigs, and a stray dingo, among others) to his freelance position catching snakes and supplying venom to Melbourne's Commonwealth Serum Laboratories in 1949, and his subsequent opening of the

Australia Reptile Park, where the Venom Program (their word choice) continues to this day.

Near the ongoing venom extraction, a wall of glass cases held habitats of various snakes. The placards of each one tried to outdo the other.

"This one is the most venomous," I said, looking at a sleek, brown taipan.

"Yeah, but this one is the deadliest," Mike replied. He stood in front of an eastern brown snake.

"If this one is the most venomous, how can that one be the deadliest?" I asked.

"Because that one is more venomous, but more people *die* from bites from this one. It has more run-ins with people."

While the deadly animals of Australia are fascinating, the more I learned about them, the more I concluded that they gave Australia an unmerited bad rap. Even with the country's wealth of snakes, spiders, saltwater crocodiles, and toxic jelly-fish, the leading cause of death is heart disease, just as it is in the United States. Whenever people tell me they would never travel to Australia because of some of its critters, I try to offer them a little perspective in that regard.

We made our way to koalas and the ubiquitous kangaroos. The setup for the kangaroos included two areas, between which the kangaroos could roam freely. In one area, people were permitted and could pet the animals. But if the kanga-roos tired of human contact, they could go past a line where people were not allowed. I liked this and felt that every mother should have a similar area, a safe zone, to which she can retreat if she needs a break.

At long last, we found the fenced area that was home to the wombat. I'm not sure how anyone could fail to see the endearing nature of the wombat. There's so much to love, from the fact that a group of these creatures is called a wisdom of wombats, to its primary defense—an exceedingly tough butt, which it uses to block predators from the entrance of its burrow.

I crouched down, and the wombat immediately came up to the fence where I stood and rubbed his back against it, encouraging me to pet him. He was, as I had hoped, the cuddliest of animals and resembled a stout little teddy bear. I wasn't sure if I was *supposed* to be petting him. The pen didn't allow visitors to enter, but at the same time, the bars of the fence were wide, and no sign prohibited the activity, to which the wombat seemed accustomed. Emilia and Ivy tentatively petted the wombat as well.

"His fur is rough," Emilia commented.

"Yeah," Ivy agreed. She withdrew her hand.

His fur was coarser than I'd imagined, though I wondered if that would have registered with me if my daughters hadn't voiced it. My adoration was great enough that I could convince myself he was soft and cuddly, an animated and affectionate teddy bear as opposed to a wild animal.

Wombats are not small animals, often weighing fifty to seventy pounds. One of the wombat's most intriguing aspects is that it has a pouch that, like the koala's, faces backward. The koala's rear-facing pouch, facilitating the consumption of the fecal pap and requiring an additional sphincter, seems unfortunate, but the wombat's is endearing, facing the rear so that when it digs a burrow, it doesn't throw a mound of dirt into its pouch and on its offspring. I found that highly considerate.

The more I pet the wombat, the more contact he seemed to want, and every now and then I flinched when I caught a glimpse of long, yellow teeth. Mike tried to get photos, but there's something slightly pathetic about a photo of contact that occurs with metal bars separating the two subjects. My hand began to feel filmy, and as I burrowed my fingers into the animal's fur, I felt grit and fleas. At which point I had to stop. Because my own waning hygiene would likely provide a wonderful environment for fleas to further colonize, and the thought of bringing fleas back into the camper, and sleeping on a flea-infested mattress for the next week and a half outweighed my long-held desire to cuddle with a wombat. As we departed, I whispered through the bars to the wombat, "I still love you."

We returned to the camper, and I once again attempted to batten everything down before we began driving.

"Aha!" I said, spotting a knife on the counter. Mike had cut slices of cheese and salami (more palatable than the ubiquitous creepy sausages) just before we'd gone inside. Come to think of it, maybe I'd reeked of salami, and that's what had drawn the wombat to me. I know that wombats are herbivores, but I also know vegetarians who don't deny the appeal of the smell of bacon. I put the knife in the sink next to my half-full water jug and looked around. I was *sure* that there was nothing left that could go flying when we started driving and shuddered to imagine a sharp knife catapulting across the camper.

We buckled in and set out. Four hours of driving lay ahead of us, and I was glad that we'd stopped for a fun activity, hoping it had worn out the girls enough that they'd sleep for the majority of the drive.

As we pulled onto the highway, nothing went flying, and I felt smug satisfaction at having finally mastered the camper. But then the road curved, and as we followed it, the entire drawer, from which the knife had come and which had been closed but not locked, flew out of the kitchen cabinet and hit the opposite wall with a terrifying crash and rain of silverware. After the initial shock and another expletive, one phrase ran through my head: *the jug is half-empty.*

* * *

Dry Is the New Clean

*At the end of my trial, I was rather hoping the judge would
send me to Australia for the rest of my life.*

—Jeffrey Archer

"Where are we heading next? Jarvis Bay?" Mike asked.
"*Jer*vis Bay. And the town is Huskisson. But it's not
Jarvis. *Jer*vis," I corrected.

"Right, Jarvis."

I let it go. Pronunciation has never been my husband's
strong suit. I'd corrected him numerous times, but he always
reverted to Jarvis. I would be mortified the next day to hear an
Australian pronounce Jervis, which sounded more like Jarvis.

We traveled south along the Princes Highway toward
Sydney, which we had every intention of going around
instead of through. I like big cities, but they are best navigated
in small cars. As we'd learned in Brisbane, driving an enormous camper through city streets was nerve-racking. Our
GPS betrayed us again, as even though we'd felt we had it
programmed to skirt the city, it instead took us to the heart
of it.

"I'm turning around," Mike said. "I don't think this is where we want to be."

I sat silent. I knew I wasn't going to be much help, so the least I could do was not increase the stress. Mike was attempting to avoid getting funneled onto a highway heading in what he thought to be the wrong direction. He turned onto a smaller road, but we continued along this with no real option for turning around to get back to what we hoped was the right direction. He turned again, down yet a smaller road, and then a smaller road. This pattern continued until he turned the camper into a narrow road that also served as the entrance to a cemetery. I am convinced that this was, hands down, the worst possible place we could have attempted to maneuver a camper van. I imagined plowing over headstones and could see the resulting headlines detailing the unimaginable disrespect of our traveling American family. I did not want to be that kind of traveler.

With an eighty-four-point turn, Mike eventually extricated us from the situation, and with a fair amount of anxiety and a few accompanying four-letter words, we finally made it south of Sydney. At our first opportunity, we stopped to stock up on alcohol. It would be hours before we could have a drink, but even the act of replenishing our stock had a calming effect, and we felt fortified to soldier on.

The drive along the Princes Highway was stunning. We traveled through picturesque towns like Berry in the Shoalhaven region of New South Wales. The coast dominated our view on the left, while beautiful hillsides, reminiscent of Ireland, stretched for miles on our right. Of course any green field in any country of the world makes me think of Ireland, and I wondered if the United States had similar features that brought it to mind for citizens of the world. Hopefully something beyond the insidious and fungus-like growth of McDonald's golden arches.

We reached Jervis Bay, found the caravan park, and were relieved to find that they could accommodate us with a powered site, despite the fact that we arrived a day ahead of our reservation.

"Your site is just here," said the clerk, a pleasant young girl who presented me with a map of the campground and its amenities. "And if you're interested, the weekly market is tomorrow. It's just a short walk." She gave me a second map, this one of the town, and circled the market location.

"Okay, maybe we'll check it out," I said.

"It's quite good," she added.

We found our site, and Mike began setting up camp while I poured drinks, needed after the day's six hours of driving.

Rainbow lorikeets flocked in groups as small as four and as large as fifty or so around the campsite. Beautiful little birds of green with blue, yellow, and red accents. Giant macaws huddled in smaller groups and at more of a distance in the treetops, but the lorikeets explored the campsite fully, not the least intimidated by humans and eager to find any crumbs left behind.

"Girls, I think it's time we shower." As fantastic as the Australian camp facilities were, at every site we visited, it still required a greater measure of work and discomfort than showering at home. The process involved Emilia and Ivy and me in a single shower stall. Usually I would begin in my bathing suit, as we often showered after walking or playing on the beach. I'd soap the girls up and rinse them off as best I could. Then they would sit, wrapped in towels, on a little bench and stare at me as I showered myself. They never grew tired of this. The grown female body was an endless wonder, and they'd make the sort of remarks you'd expect, like "Why do you have hair down there?" to which I would reply that at puberty, all humans grow hair in certain areas. This provoked shrieks of disgust and the assertions that they had absolutely no intention of ever doing so themselves. Other inquiries involved my breasts (and differentiating between breasts and nipples), my C-section scar (which would lead to further discussions of how babies are made and the two means by which they exit the mother's body), and of course, the scar on my back that for some reason my daughters find reminiscent of poultry. But not all questions left me feeling like I was teaching a sixth-grade health class or that I resembled a chicken nugget, and their favorite part of watching me shower was when I washed my face.

"Watch, Ivy. Here she goes," Emilia would whisper excitedly.

"She's going to put soap right on her *face*," Ivy replied.

"How do you *do* that, Mama?" Emilia asked.

"And now she's going to let water hit her right on her face. All over!" Ivy added.

Showering with my daughters was both entertaining and exhausting, and I longed for the day when I would once again be able to do so in private. After showering, we dressed, but nearly everything we had was damp—a combination of the rain, washed clothes not being given the opportunity to properly dry, and two gallons of water flying through the air of our camper. I decided that sometimes showering was overrated and that just being dry should be the new goal. So dry became the new clean.

The next morning, we found a store and purchased a toaster. The toaster that came with the camper had what appeared to be melted plastic adhered to the top of it, which didn't make me excited about using it.

"What other food do we need?" I asked Mike.

"Can we get some sort of meat?" Mike asked. "I'm feeling kind of deprived."

"Sure," I said, and decided that with some mince (what we know as ground beef) and a few canned items, I could whip up a pot of chili in the camper.

We left the grocery store and strolled through downtown. The day hadn't yet heated up, and we decided to splurge on coffee. We'd been making do with instant coffee thus far on our trip, and a real cup of coffee, or even a cappuccino, sounded heavenly. We stopped at a restaurant along the shoreline that offered coffee and smoothies and a fairly impressive menu. I ordered a cappuccino, and we waited for a good fifteen minutes before it was ready. Mike and I kept looking at each other, saying, "This is going to be the best cappuccino we've *ever had.*" Which is how we stay excited when our order is forgotten or delayed, which seems to happen to us a lot. While we waited, he studied one of the restaurant's flyers advertising that later that night would be Vegetarian Mexican Night.

"Look, Amanda," he said. "This sounds really good. Maybe we should come back here for dinner." The part that intrigued him was "Mexican," not "Vegetarian." If Mike had to pick one country's food to survive on, I'm sure he'd opt for Mexico.

"No!" I said. And I saw his face register shock at my vehemence. Of course, I would have loved to attend Mexican Vegetarian Night, which to my ears was a delightful combination of words. But we had other plans. "I just bought everything to make chili. Twenty minutes ago, you were complaining that your carnivorous nature wasn't being nurtured, and now you want to go to vegetarian night?"

"Chili sounds wonderful, sweetie."

"You're damn right it does."

"Try this." Our cappuccino was ready, and he took it from the counter and handed it to me as a physical means of changing the subject. "It's going to be the best cappuccino we've ever had."

And it was.

Back at the camper, we plugged in our new toaster and decided that toast was the most wonderful food on the planet. If you survive for an extended period of time on Ramen, peanut butter and jelly sandwiches, apples, and bananas, it doesn't take much to suddenly blow your mind and your taste buds. Toast did the trick. How had we denied ourselves the sophisticated treat of toasted bread?

"You want to go check out the market?" I asked Mike after we'd fully fortified ourselves with carbohydrates. "The girl in the office said it's not far and it's really good."

"Do you want to?" he countered.

"Heck yeah. Remember how awesome that Eumundi market was?" His eyes lit up. "I am *not* trying on any more bathing suits," I added, and he resumed his previous expression. "But I definitely want to go."

Forty minutes later, we were drenched in sweat.

"I just want to go back to the camper," Ivy pleaded, close to tears.

"Man, it's hot," Mike said.

"We've got to be close," I reasoned.

"I hope it's worth it."

"It will be."

When we finally arrived, the first stall we came upon sold a variety of items, possibly used, sheathed in dusty plastic. There were toilet seat covers, clown wigs, bras, shower curtain rings, pantyhose, and toenail clippers. And when I say shower curtain rings, I don't mean that they took a household object and turned it into a work of art by carving the rings from Tasmanian birch and imprinting Indigenous Australian art on them. No, these were shower curtain rings. Plastic, beige, shower curtain rings. Made in China.

"Oh my god, I'm so sorry," I muttered.

"What are you sorry for?" Mike asked.

"I'm sorry that we walked three miles in stifling heat with two children under the age of ten to reach a flea market."

"Yep."

We walked around further and found that there were *some* interesting artisan stalls where people sold higher-quality items. We bought fruit from a vendor and a copy of *Black Beauty* from a bin of used books for Emilia. A man played a pan flute. Another, dressed as a terribly unconvincing Santa, handed out lollipops to children, and only later would it occur to me to question his affiliation and motive.

We paid a few dollars for the kids to have three minutes in a bouncy house, because we needed to lift their spirits in order to survive the walk back to the caravan park. I wondered what it was about the market that the campground clerk thought merited the description of "quite good." Perhaps she hadn't been to any other markets—or she lived a fairly rural life and appreciated the social nature of the event. Or maybe she's an avid fan of the pan flute.

Huskisson *was* a good town for riding bikes. A paved path wound miles along the shore, so the following day we sought out a bike rental shop. We rented two adult bikes. One had a tagalong attached, which essentially creates a tandem bike, the rear seat being smaller for a child. To the other adult bike we attached a small trailer with a seat for another child. We rode the bikes back to the camper where we added a cooler filled with snacks, water, and Toohey's New, the beer to which we'd grown affectionately accustomed.

As we set out along the path, I huffed as quietly as I could, pretending that the ride was as effortless for me as it appeared to be for my husband. I was thankful when, just a few minutes after beginning the journey, we were forced to dismount and walk the bikes across the narrow bridge over Moona Moona Creek. As we rode, we admired the houses along the shoreline and stopped periodically to drink a beer on the narrow stretch of sand known as Collingwood Beach. This was the reward for having exerted myself on a bicycle, as I'm not confident or competent when it comes to navigating on two wheels. But while an occasional beer may increase my confidence, it has the opposite effect with regard to my competency.

In Vincentia, we left the bike path in favor of the easier ride along Elizabeth Drive and eventually made our way to Plantation Point, where a park offered shade and a playground.

"Ooh," Ivy said. "Can we play?"

"Yes, go for it."

"But why is your face so red?"

"Because riding a bike is hard," I explained.

"It's not *that* hard," she said.

I bit my tongue regarding the fact that Ivy does not know how to ride a bike.

"It *is* when you're towing a trailer with a five-year-old inside," I huffed.

"Your face looks like a tomato," she said, before running to join her sister on the playground. It's unfortunate but true. Exercise makes me look like a giant tomato for a full hour after I've stopped. This, combined with the fact that I sweat to a greater extent than most people, makes me a less than desirable workout buddy.

After the girls played for a bit, we walked down to the beach and spent an hour exploring and collecting shells before returning to the bikes. Halfway through the return trip, I was again in need of a break and called up ahead to Mike to let him know. He pulled the tandem bike over. The path was right along the beach at that point, and Mike unknowingly stopped just a few feet from a woman who was happily sunbathing and apparently trying to avoid any tan lines from the waist up. I stopped next to Mike, with the intention of whispering to him that perhaps we should go a bit further, but I was preempted by Ivy, who used the pause in action to clarify a few things.

"So, Mommy," she said. "The big thing is the breast, and just the little thing is the pimple? Wait, I mean the nipple," she corrected herself loudly. Ivy didn't see the woman, and it was mere coincidence that she used that moment to revisit anatomy questions sprouting from our recent shower experience. But the woman on the beach, if she heard our conversation, wouldn't know that.

I was the only member of our four-person party to spot the topless sunbather, and my family looked confused when, after asking for a break, I muttered, "Of all the places to stop," and pedaled ahead.

* * *

After two days in Huskisson, I decided to log on to the Internet, which I'd been neglecting for most of our trip. I found a commotion on Facebook, which included a fair amount of concern for my well-being, including such comments as "You're not in Sydney, are you? Are you???" and "Let us know you're safe."

"Passed Sydney two days ago," I reassured my friends. "We're fine."

I logged onto the news then to find out their reason for concern. They called it the Siege of Sydney and claimed a radical Muslim was holding hostages in a coffee shop. I wanted to believe that my friends on Facebook were overreacting. The "siege" was *probably* blown wildly out of proportion. It was likely a big misunderstanding. A peaceful protest of some sort that had gotten slightly out of hand. But the next day, we woke to news that that was not the case. Innocent people had been killed. The murderer had a history of violent crime, including pending charges of accessory to the murder of his ex-wife, fraud, and a "spiritual healing" business in which his healing techniques required vulnerable women to be naked and molested.

In response to the news, I closed my computer, and Emilia and I wandered over to a family who was feeding the lorikeets. We made small talk. They were from Lebanon, and from their dress, I assumed Muslim. Our kids were similar ages. We didn't talk about the news, and I wanted nothing more than the innocence and friendliness of our interaction to counteract everything I'd read about the recent tragedy. We'd encountered handfuls of Muslim families vacationing along the coast, and from body language alone, I concluded that Muslim and non-Muslim relations in Australia operated under the same strain as they do in the United States. In the simple acts of feeding birds and making friendly conversation, our two families rejected fear and bigotry and fanaticism. It was a lovely moment and one for which I am grateful. Sydney seemed a world away.

The next morning, we readied to depart and head further south to yet another campsite. I collected our shells that had been placed in the sun to dry and gave them each the sniff test. If they reeked, they would be left behind. If not, they would continue with us on our journey.

"Mom, can I please feed the lorikeets before we go?" Emilia said.

"I'm going inside," Ivy declared.

"Me too," agreed Mike. They had no desire for an encounter with the birds.

Emilia and I sat on the grass, quiet and still, each holding a slice of pear. Within minutes, we were surrounded. Lorikeets sat on our arms, laps, and shoulders and ate from our hands. I shuddered to think what our clothes would look like once we stood up, and I wondered how much extra laundry I'd created for myself by allowing my daughter and me to be covered in bird shit. But with the delicate yet noisy creatures feasting on pears, hopping around and on us, we felt giddy. We loved the birds.

Then one bird mounted another.

"Whoa," said Emilia. "What are they doing?"

"Uh, they're actually mating," I said.

"Mating?"

"Yeah, so the female can lay eggs and make more lorikeets."

"Oh man." She stared at the birds intently, one roughly having its way with the other. "I can't wait to see the baby," she said, as if a tiny baby lorikeet might materialize at any minute.

Eventually the pears were gone and a few birds remained, content to be near us, while the majority moved on in search of other campers with forgotten or offered food. We stood and tentatively surveyed ourselves and the camp chairs. I didn't find a single dropping. Had the birds intuited that campers were more likely to feed them if they didn't get crapped on in the process? Or did these mysterious creatures produce invisible excrement? Either way, I didn't care, and it made the birds all the more likable.

* * *

Killers in Eden

*For thousands of years, killer whales have hunted
the great baleen whales in every ocean on earth, yet only in one place
have they ever co-operated with humans to hunt whales,
and then largely with only one family, the Davidsons.*

—KillersofEden.com

Murramarang was another word I found both intriguing and beautiful, but one that I could only pronounce in clunky delivery, never quite sure on which syllable to rest the accent. Our campsite at Murramarang National Park butted right up against the beach but was also surrounded by protected forest. The scene was, like many we encountered along the Australian coast, idyllic. The campsite included a playground, about which the girls were ecstatic, and as they played on the swings or climbed the equipment, wild kangaroos napped in the shade on the playground, undeterred by the presence of these tiny humans. Kangaroos were so plentiful on the playground that when we'd checked in, camp information included a plea to campers to not feed the kangaroos. "Especially bread," it read, which apparently campers are apt to do.

We explored the surroundings, beginning with the beach. As we emerged onto the coast, we were once again faced with a magnificent backdrop where only a few other people strolled. A woman with her head covered in a hijab held her phone up in front of her, trying to get a selfie with the water behind her.

"Would you like me to take your picture?" I asked.

"Oh yes." She smiled brightly. "I just love the water."

I took a few photos of her with her phone while Mike wandered ahead with the girls.

"Are you American?" she asked.

"Yes. We're here for two months traveling around."

"How is your trip going? Do you like it here?" There was a girlish exuberance about her, as if there was nothing more that she wanted at that moment than to stand on the beach with me and discuss the wonders of Australia.

"Yes, of course. We absolutely love it here."

"Well, can't you just move here then?" she asked. Her excitement and girlish naiveté was endearing, and I hoped it wouldn't be tinged in the days to come with the increasing tensions of Muslim-Australian relations, which we'd noted in comments and glances toward Muslims long before the tragedy of the Siege of Sydney.

"We like our home too," I said. "But yes, Australia is wonderful."

"Well, thank you for taking my picture." She smiled.

"You're welcome." I smiled back, then turned to catch up with my family.

"Girls, look at this place," Mike said, gesturing to the beach, forest, and tiny outcrop of islands.

"No, Dad, look at this stick we found," said Emilia, and she and Ivy held a twelve-foot stick aloft over their heads. The beach was beautiful, but so were all of the other beaches they'd seen, and they'd never seen a stick quite like this one before.

We walked along the beach until it ended abruptly in a steep rocky area.

"Okay, should we head back then?" I asked. Ivy and I turned back in the direction of camp.

"Let's keep going," Mike said.

"Yeah," Emilia agreed. "Let's climb."

"I don't know." I surveyed the steep rock. Ivy looked doubtful too.

"Come on," Mike said.

"Adventure is out there," Emilia added.

Ivy and I survived the trek despite flip-flops and beach attire, though with notably less enthusiasm than Mike and Emilia. At the top, we headed slightly inland and continued on a trail leading through the forest. I noticed that both Mike and I traveled more cautiously than we had on previous forest walks, keeping the girls close by, and I knew with certainty that our caution was a direct result of having visited the Australian Reptile Park and the snakes and spiders that called the land home. Mike walked with a stick and occasionally prodded the ground before he stepped. Emilia picked up a hiking stick at one point as well.

"Daddy and I are alike because we both have sticks," Emilia said.

"Well, Mommy and I are alike because we both go potty a lot," Ivy countered.

In the forest, we encountered two troops of kangaroos. These were more cautious and wary than the kangaroos that lazed about the campsite. We'd spot them and remain still for a few minutes, staring at them, until the kangaroos darted through the trees to find a more secluded spot.

"Hey, girls, look," I whispered, pointing through the brush

at a lone, still animal hunched over.

"What is it you think you're looking at?" asked Mike.

At that point, I realized that I'd been observing a stump, though a tree stump does have one advantage over a real kangaroo in that it is much easier to photograph.

At the campsite that afternoon, I took a postcard-worthy photo of an upright kangaroo staring directly at me, with the head of a good-sized joey also visible from the confines of his mother's pouch.

"These kangaroos sure are friendly," I said. "I just got an amazing picture of one. It practically posed for me."

"That's why they're friendly," Mike said, and motioned to a nearby campsite where we watched a family feed the kangaroos an entire loaf of bread. Apparently this family also eschews brochures and guidelines.

"Oh no," someone cried from yet a different site. "They got into the mangoes!"

"The kangaroos aren't necessarily *friendly*," Mike clarified. "They're *hungry*."

A little boy who belonged to the rule-breaking bread-givers began chasing ducks around menacingly. I decided I did not like that little boy, not one bit. For all we knew, there could have been a flea-free wisdom of wombats waiting to stroll into camp to cuddle with us, but his atrocious behavior had prevented the wisdom from doing so. I silently dubbed the boy "Little Shit."

The showers at this campsite required a dollar to use, and as we were there for only one night, I decided to skip it. There is no logic in this thinking. One Australian dollar is equivalent to approximately eighty cents, and yet that eighty cents prohibited me from bathing myself and my children. But it wasn't frugality alone that made me eschew the facilities. There was also the time factor. When you bought your shower, you purchased a few minutes. I panicked at the thought of water ceasing while I had soap in my eyes. Bathing should not be a speed sport. By that point, I'd also come to accept the fact that no matter how often we showered, life in the camper would always feel grubby.

"I think I'm going to skip the shower tonight," I said.

"I think I'm going to go for a run on the beach," Mike said.

"You just had to one-up me, didn't you?"

"Yep."

Our diet included such favorites as veggies and hummus but also a substantial amount of alcohol and, of course, peanut butter and jelly sandwiches. As a result, we felt atrophy setting in, combined with the acquisition of an extra layer of fat on our bodies. We needed exercise, beyond a single beer-accompanied bike ride. Mike returned after half an hour, sweaty, breathing hard, and with a rugged handsomeness to his face that no one would ever describe as a big red tomato.

The next day, we continued south along the Princes Highway to Eden, which would be our last stop in New South Wales before heading west into Victoria on our journey to Melbourne. By this point, I was positively giddy at the thought of returning the camper to the rental company.

We avoided killing an echidna crossing the road in a slow lumber, passed more wineries at which we did not stop, and more billboards warning that sleep equaled death. At one point, we passed a dead wombat on the side of the road, and I was glad that the girls' seats were too low for them to have seen out the window. The wombat was on its back, four legs sticking straight up in the air. It was a clean accident, as far as roadkill goes, without any visible blood. The animal resembled a large teddy bear reaching up for a hug.

Eden was home to the Killer Whale Museum, which sounded like a place worth stopping and at the same time brought to mind every nature show I've seen of killer whales tossing seals about or snacking on penguins. The reality of what we found at the museum was far more brutal.

Between 1840 and 1930, a pod of killer whales worked in tandem with human whalers, and Eden's Killer Whale Museum largely serves as a memorial to the most famous killer whale of the group, Old Tom. The killer whales would herd a baleen whale into Twofold Bay and alert the Davidsons, a whaling family, with some strategically placed tail slapping on the water's surface. The whalers would rush to their boats, employ their harpoons, and finish the job. It seems like an interesting and unlikely partnership between orcas and humans, almost quaint, until you consider it from the whale's point of view. Two apex predators joining forces hardly seems like a fair fight. When the whale was dead, the orcas would have a night to feast on the tongue and lips, the only parts they were interested in, and the whalers referred to this arrangement as the Law of the Tongue, after which the humans could begin harvesting the blubber.

Old Tom's skeleton is on display, and he is presented with incredible reverence, a beloved mascot of the area. In September of 1930, the *Eden Magnet* published a sizable obituary for the "Orca Gladiator" and described him as "renowned in war," which I thought was quite a stretch for describing a predator hunting prey. By the time we left Eden, I was convinced that, for the most part, killer whales and humans are a bunch of assholes.

We traveled to Nowa Nowa, where we'd booked a night at a caravan park for our final stay in the camper. The previous weeks of moving from campsite to campsite, feeling filthy and unable to keep my surroundings clean, left me short-tempered and grubby and fully aware of the fact that I'm not nearly as tough as I think I am. My husband and children are far more adaptable and capable of handling such situations. Mike did join me in longing for real food, though, and we agreed that once we were settled, we'd splurge on a restaurant. The peanut butter and jelly and gas station food had grown tiresome. It was interesting that while I would not stop at any fast-food restaurant, I was completely okay with buying food from a gas station.

As we left New South Wales and the GPS led us deeper into Victoria, I yawned as we approached a billboard that said, "Yawning?" It seemed a bit of highway kismet. Underneath the huge question, it reminded me that "A microsleep can kill."

"I think you're supposed to turn up here," I said.

"Are you sure? This doesn't look right."

"Well, that's what the GPS is telling me."

"Okay," he said skeptically and turned off of Princes Highway onto a dirt road. A few trailers dotted the area, but not like a campsite, more like trailers on small plots of land where I imagined generations of people being raised alongside broken vehicles, discarded appliances, and outdoor couches. The road took us in a large arc that led us back to Princes Highway, with no caravan park in sight. With every turn, the GPS tried to recalculate and direct us to a route that seemed not to exist.

"I think we need to try that other road back there," I said.

"I don't think that's right either," Mike said.

If I had thought rationally about the situation, I would have said, "You're right. Where do you think we should go?" And then supported whatever Mike said wholeheartedly. Because in our decades-long history together, when we've disagreed about the direction of things, I have been right three times, while Mike has been correct the other ninety-eight billion times. But for some reason, he decided to humor me and pulled down a different dirt road, at the end of which he was certain no campsite awaited.

Our oversized vehicle lumbered down the narrow road of dirt and rock, and I distinctly remembered signing a document on which we promised only to take the vehicle on paved roads. This was not the sort of recreational vehicle meant for off-road exploring. We traveled slowly for three miles, Mike growing more certain this was the wrong way with each passing second, while I desperately clung to the hope that around the next bend civilization and hot showers would appear. Around the next bend, a chain hung across the road prohibiting any further travel. I groaned.

"Okay then," Mike said, and that was the extent of his gloating on the matter of having been right, yet again. "I guess we'll have to turn around."

This was no easy task because the road was narrow and bordered on either side by a small ditch. Mike executed a twelve-point turn, and the camper creaked with each minuscule adjustment, as if the vehicle was audibly protesting having been driven to such a place.

We're going to break the camper, I thought. *We've come this far, and we're going to break it with only one night to go.* My heart jumped at the sound of a loud pop, and while it must have been the cracking of a rock under our tires, I was sure that we had indeed broken the vehicle, and I wondered how many thousands of dollars we'd have to pay for whatever damage we were doing. As we traveled back the three miles to the main road, I was sure the camper would stop working at any moment and refuse to take us any farther. But at least we'd live, because as miserable as I was having spent weeks in the camper, it offered us basic amenities and excellent shelter if we were in a survival situation.

And then I smelled something odd, not the usual stink I'd grown accustomed to of having a toilet in your vehicle, but a different smell, a chemical smell, and I was sure we'd done some damage to the vehicle that was releasing a deadly odorless gas into the air, which would kill us all. It doesn't matter that when I smell something odd, I always think of it as a deadly odorless gas. I'm sure I can smell something that can't be smelled, and that when I smell it, that means my entire family is about to pass out. Like in the movies when you see a half second of realization on someone's face before an entire room of people collapses.

We didn't collapse (it's possible the smell was a manifestation of my paranoia and hypochondria), and the camper kept chugging along, but we never did find the campsite. And though we'd made a reservation and paid a deposit, we discontinued the search. We wanted to get out of the area we were in, which held little more than dilapidated trailers and a gas station. There was a depressed air about the place, contrary to the happy and relaxed Australia we'd come to love.

We continued on to Lakes Entrance and pulled into a quiet park that had plenty of vacancies, a small pool, and a playground next to a fish cleaning station. A short walk to the back of the grounds revealed that while we were situated along

AK TURNER

the shore, adjacent to 90 Mile Beach, we were also on a cliff top. We navigated a long staircase down to the water's edge, and for the first time, our view of the water included the Bass Strait, which we would cross in our journey from the mainland to Tasmania.

"That was a lot of stairs," Ivy said when we reached the beach.

"And we'll have to go back up all the stairs," Emilia said.

Ivy gave me a look of horror, and her eyes pleaded with me to say it wasn't so.

"It's true, Ivy, but you can do it."

"And," Mike added, "tonight we're going to eat at a *restaurant!*"

"Yay," Ivy cheered.

"This is going to be the best night ever," Emilia agreed.

When we checked in, I asked about restaurants and was informed that a lovely restaurant called the Waterwheel was nearby, within walking distance, and it even had a van that would take us to and from the restaurant, if we liked. This sounded ideal, and the woman at check-in spoke glowingly of the food, which was all I needed. We decided to walk to the restaurant, and then we'd take their shuttle back. Before we left, I scrubbed my face and even went so far as to put on a little makeup.

"Wow, Mom, are you wearing makeup?" Ivy asked loudly as we walked through the camp to the road that would lead us to the restaurant.

"Shh, but yes."

"Mom, I can see your makeup," Emilia bellowed. And the fact that my children were so startled by my appearance told me just how rough I'd looked in the preceding weeks. There was also the possibility that in the dim light of the camper, I'd done a poor job of makeup application and in the light of day looked clown-like, something I suspect I've been guilty of on occasion.

At the restaurant, emboldened by the camp clerk's glowing endorsement of the Waterwheel's food, we looked the menu over, and Mike and I decided to fully splurge by ordering the giant seafood platter for two, while the kids opted for fish and chips. The food arrived with expert presentation. The girls' fish and chips looked downright gourmet, while the waitress presented Mike and me with a three-tiered tower of various types of seafood.

"Wow," I exclaimed.

"This looks awesome," Mike said.

We dug in, and with each bite, the table quieted, not because we were so engrossed with our food but because everything was either devoid of flavor or tasted fishy, which is ironically not how you want to describe a fish you're eating. Our three-tiered seafood extravaganza was an expensive disappointment.

"This is really awful," Mike said.

"Maybe the kids' food is better," I ventured and swiped a bite from Ivy's plate. "Yeah, that's pretty awful too."

"Mom," Emilia said, "I'm just not hungry."

"Me, neither," Ivy agreed.

"Just eat as much as you want, kids," I instructed. "We'll have some snacks when we get back to the camper." I will not be forced to eat bad food, so I'm certainly not going to make my children do so. We paid for our food and took the shuttle back to the campsite where I made peanut butter and jelly sandwiches, and, truth be told, they were delicious.

* * *

Take My Keys

It destroys one's nerves to be amiable all day.

– Benjamin Disraeli

"Now remember, girls, when we go get the car, you are going to stay in the camper, and *don't* speak," I commanded.

"Got it," they chimed.

We were driving the camper to a home in a Melbourne suburb where we would meet the owner of an old Camry for rent. Then we'd return the camper, and the following day, we'd take the Camry on the ferry to Tasmania for the remainder of our trip. Tasmania is a state of Australia, just like Victoria or New South Wales, but unlike those regions, it is also its own island. There hadn't been any specific language in the rental agreement prohibiting taking the rental car as far as Tasmania, but we still felt it was a part of our itinerary of which the owner didn't necessarily need to be apprised. And in the preceding month, Emilia had informed the majority of the population of mainland Australia that we were headed to

Tasmania; I wanted to make sure she put that practice on hold in the presence of the Camry's owner.

We found the home and spotted an old white Camry out front. The girls dutifully remained in the camper while Mike and I approached the house. The owner came out, a slight, nervous man named Peter. Unlike the previous car we'd rented, where the owners gleefully handed over their keys, as well as their lizard, Peter painstakingly walked us through every line of the paperwork, took photographs of every inch of the car, and made sure we signed in triplicate. Our instinct to keep Emilia unheard and out of sight had been a good one, in light of Peter's nervous nature and apparent affection for the Camry. Ironically, Peter's car was also a piece of crap on four wheels, whereas the previous car we'd rented was a dream by comparison.

When Peter was finally satisfied and handed over the keys to his Camry, Mike looked at me and said, "Do you want me to pull the car out for you?"

"Uh, I think I have it," I said. I would have to drive the car through Melbourne, following Mike to the place where we needed to return the camper. The idea that I would do that but needed Mike to pull the car out of a straight driveway was ridiculous. But I hadn't driven on the other side of the road from the other side of the car in a few weeks, and I think Mike wanted to ease me into the situation. Also, he probably felt Peter would feel calmer if the last thing he saw was a man getting into the driver's seat of his car as opposed to a woman, an idea to which I could only respond, *Fuck that.*

Our plan worked as intended, with one substantial oversight. Our walkie-talkies were not charged, meaning that I would have to follow Mike, but if we got separated, we would have no means of communication. If I did lose his trail, all I knew was that I needed to meet up with him at the caravan rental company in Footscray. Even if I had to stop for directions a million times, I figured I could eventually get there working with this knowledge alone.

Mike drove the camper, and I tailgated him as best as I could without actually plowing the Camry into his rear. At a busy intersection, he waited for a break in oncoming traffic so that he could turn right. As he waited for his opening, his signal changed to a red arrow, but I could tell that he didn't see it, as he continued to inch the camper forward.

"No," I screamed in the Camry. "Red arrow, red arrow!" And I watched as he inched the camper forward, beginning to turn just as a new wave of traffic came to life and headed his way. "Red arrow!" I yelled, despite the certainty that there was no possible way for my voice to be heard. It might have been an attempt at telepathy on my part. He abruptly stopped and avoided collision. And I desperately hoped we wouldn't have any similar instances, as wrecking the camper on our way to return it would put a bit of a damper on the day. In addition to avoiding catastrophe, the fact that he didn't leave me behind was good, as I didn't want to spend the next three hours driving around Melbourne asking which way it was to Footscray.

Footscray, it turned out, was a white-knuckled forty-five minutes from Peter's home. I was nervous about staying on Mike's tail while traversing through a big city and apprehensive for Mike, driving the uncomfortably large beast without a copilot. But eventually we reached Footscray, found the rental return, and parked both vehicles. I immediately went inside and waited in line, keys in hand.

"Shouldn't we move all of our stuff to the car first?" Mike asked. But I was so desperate to rid us of the camper, I wanted to hand over the keys before doing anything else.

I waited in line behind a well-dressed, exceedingly clean couple. They were inquiring about renting a camper in the coming year. After a few minutes, I realized that what appeared to me to be an elevated standard of hygiene was really just basic personal care, but when compared to the layers of filth on my body, the gap in our appearances seemed large. One exception was the man's toenails, visible as he wore flip-flops (I couldn't ever warm up to the notion of calling them thongs, as Australians do, because then I would inevitably picture the man in a thong). He had long toes but even longer toenails, thick and yellow and almost weapon-like in appearance. I wanted him to put on shoes. I wanted to introduce them to the Internet so that they could research and plan their trip online instead of here, which forced me to wait in line. When they finally went on their way, a plethora of brochures in hand, I practically hurled the keys at the man behind the counter. "We're returning a vehicle," I said.

"But we still need to move our stuff out of it," Mike added.

"Oh," the man said, "well do that first and *then* come see me." He pushed the keys back across the counter at me.

I looked at them as if they carried disease, then reluctantly picked them up again. We went back to the parking lot and began the substantial task of moving all of our belongings from the camper into the Camry. We finally returned the camper, informing the man of the leak in the shower and failed coupling of the gray water hose. He reimbursed us for the price of the toaster and asked us how our trip had been.

"It was an adventure," I said.

"I'm sure it was," he responded and offered something between a smile and a smirk, no doubt inspired by our haggard and road-weary appearances.

With all of our belongings now crammed into the Camry, we set out to find our hotel, the Great Southern Hotel, and I was sure that it would, indeed, be great. Not only would we sleep on a real mattress, but I would be afforded the luxury of showering alone. Before bed, I'd have a normal sink and plenty of clean water—the temperature of which would be at my discretion—with which to wash my face and brush my teeth. I could use the toilet and not later have to empty the contents, a task which, as distasteful as it was, everyone should have to do at some point in their life. Just as I feel that everyone who eats meat should be forced at some point to butcher an animal.

I didn't regret the camper experience, but I was glad it had come to a close. And for all of its minor inconveniences, I was well aware of the fact that I couldn't claim we'd actually been roughing it. Roughing it doesn't include electricity and mattresses, a toaster and a mini-fridge, or a flat-screen television. It's embarrassing to admit, but yes, our camper had a flat-screen television, and while Mike and I never watched it, it was regularly employed in the entertainment of our children.

We located the Great Southern Hotel, and I thought Great was maybe a bit of a stretch. We checked in to find that the parking garage was full, and they directed us to another one nearby. When we reached our room, it was the laughable sort. A window facing a brick wall, threadbare carpet.

"They don't even have a bedspread," Mike noted.

"Maybe that's not such a bad thing," I said. I figured the less fabric there was, the less real estate for potential cooties to inhabit.

"I love it here," said Ivy.

"This place is *beautiful,*" Emilia added.

"Don't get too comfy, girls," Mike instructed. "I want to get out of this room."

As we left, we saw a flood of people coming down the hall toward us. Adults and children who had a few of the adjacent rooms, and I smiled at them offhandedly, happy at the mere sight of a group of families.

On the street, Mike suggested we go in the direction of what looked like a busy, central area. We headed that way to find that the area he'd seen was busy, but that was because it was a train station. I love trains and train stations but only if we're traveling. Otherwise, it feels like going to the airport to hang out but not board a plane. I'm sure there are people who do that, but I don't want to be one of them.

We weren't interested in seeing *all* that Melbourne has to see. We had only one evening before heading to Tasmania, and after Tasmania we'd have three full days to explore Melbourne, so we delayed any tourist inclinations. Our goals were reduced to food and killing time outside of the Great Southern Hotel. Mike fiddled with his phone for a few minutes, then said, "We should head this way." He led us to increasingly desolate streets. From the busy train station where a thousand people scurried, we now found ourselves walking block after block without another person to be seen.

"Are you sure we should head this way?" I asked.

"Yes, just trust me," he said, and I knew that I should.

"Mommy, where are we going?" Ivy asked.

"I don't know," I admitted.

Not only were the streets vacant, but the few restaurants and other businesses we passed were closed, despite the fact that it was coming up to five o'clock in the evening on a Saturday. After another block, we saw a few signs of life, then Mike blurted, "There! That's where we're going!" He pointed to a second-story sign on a building that read "Vapiano."

"My hero," I said. Everyone was tired and had grown increasingly unsettled by the desolate streets, but the prospect of pasta and wine makes everything better. We had an incredible meal for half the price of the atrocious seafood platter from the night before at the Waterwheel, and I felt that all was right with the world. I was glad that Mike had identified Vapiano without telling me about it. Had I looked at their website, I might have read how the restaurant describes itself: "like a hairy chest sporting a gold medallion—smart, yet casual."

With reluctance, we returned to the Great Southern Hotel. We turned in early, partly because I wanted to make sure we left early in the morning and weren't late for the ferry to Tasmania, but mostly because when you're sharing a hotel room with two little girls whose bedtime is 8:30, you can't exactly stay up late and party. I'd picked the hotel because it was just a few miles from the ferry terminal. We would get an early start. If we missed the boat, there wouldn't be an opportunity to catch another one on another day, as the ferry was booked solid over the coming Christmas holidays. Our Tasmanian adventure depended on that ferry.

As we settled in to sleep, I heard the loud stomping of feet through the not-so-soundproof walls of the Great Southern Hotel. This was followed by running and slamming of doors, all courtesy of the families we'd seen when we first checked in. The clock showed that it was well past nine, but the running and slamming continued. I find that when you're in another country, you'll often tolerate more, because you don't want to assert yourself too much in customs and a culture that you might not fully understand. But the children wreaking havoc in the halls of the hotel at night, running from room to room and slamming doors every few seconds, was too much. As my blood hovered just short of a rolling boil, I threw back the pathetic excuse for covers.

"Amanda," Mike advised, "don't do it."

"Sorry, there's no stopping me on this one." I opened the door to the hallway, and three children, ranging from ages five to ten, stopped in their tracks and looked at me. "Where are your parents?" I demanded. No one responded. "Where are your parents?" Maybe it was the American accent or the fury obviously inside of me, but they seemed stunned into silence. I turned to one of the hotel rooms from which they'd been running laps and pounded on the door. Another small child opened it, but an older teenager emerged from behind him. "Where are their parents?" I demanded of her.

"They're not here," she said meekly. The parents had gone out for the evening, and as I understood it, this girl was in charge of the plentiful and rambunctious brood. She looked frightened of me, which briefly made me wonder what I looked like. I hadn't glanced in the mirror before setting out on this crusade.

"Well, this has to *stop*," I hissed. "This is ridiculous." My words were anything but fierce, but the manner in which I spoke them made up for it. I returned to my room and slept comfortably in the silence of the hotel the rest of the night.

* * *

The Spirit of Tasmania

*For families and children, taking your own car is easy and
convenient—especially given all the extra luggage you need.
Just make sure the cricket set is easy to find ...*

—TheSpiritOfTasmania.com

We woke in plenty of time to make it to the ferry. The
hotel was just a few miles from the dock, and I planned
to have us there well before the cutoff time of 9:15 when, as
my reservation warned me, no further boarding would be
allowed as the ship prepared for its ten o'clock departure. This
type of warning scares me into a state of minute-by-minute
planning, and in this situation, when a forfeited reservation
would mean we wouldn't get to Tasmania at *all*, the pressure
was on. I hadn't flown 7,192 miles and lived in a camper for
two weeks traveling another 1,386 miles down the coast and
braved the horror that is the Great Southern Hotel only to be
denied my Tasmanian experience. I would be on that ship.

As we left the (not so) Great Southern Hotel and walked to
the nearby parking garage, I glanced again at our ferry reservation. Beyond the warning about not being late, there was
another warning that if you were bringing a vehicle aboard,

which we were, you must be able to show registration. When we'd acquired the car, I didn't recall any registration papers but figured them to be tucked away in the glove box. We reached the car and packed it to the gills once again with all of our belongings and random acquired items like hot sauce and hand soap. The girls sleepily buckled themselves in back, and I immediately went for the glove box to check for registration papers. It was empty.

"This ferry reservation says we need to have the car's registration," I said.

"What?"

"But I don't see anything anywhere."

"And we're just talking about this now?"

"Well, yes," I said. "Now is when we're talking about it. This is now."

A frantic fifteen minutes ensued of searching for our rental agreement, in the hopes that it would suffice in the face of a lack of official registration papers. You'd think that when all of your possessions fit into one crappy Camry, locating a piece of paper wouldn't be that difficult. There are a limited number of cubic feet within which said paper can possibly be. But stress causes you to question which areas you've searched and which you haven't, resulting in looking through the same stack of papers three times, while neglecting a different stack, which is invariably home to the particular paper for which you are searching.

"Here it is!" I yelled triumphantly.

"The registration?" Mike asked hopefully.

"No, the rental agreement."

He scowled in response.

"Can we just go now?" I snapped. Mike was annoyed that

I hadn't addressed this issue sooner. I was annoyed with him for being annoyed at me, which no doubt annoyed him. And now we'd cut into our buffer time.

I felt my heart pounding as we drove to the ferry terminal and found ourselves within a mile of the ferry but at the end of a line of cars. Two roads fed into the terminal, and both were backed up and barely moving. The ferry holds hundreds of cars, and we were one in a sea of many. We inched closer, and I stared at the dashboard clock, which mocked me as 9:15 came and went. Still, they seemed to be allowing cars to continue on the ferry, and we could do nothing but go forward and hope for the best. When we finally made it into the first set of gates, I felt we might actually reach Tasmania. We proceeded forth at a crawl to customs, when I realized that a banana sat between the driver and passenger seats, this contraband of fruit for which customs would surely chastise me and return me to quarantine. I was already on their watch list.

"Hurry, everyone, eat!" I commanded, peeling the banana.

"But I'm not hungry." Emilia yawned.

I saw that yawn as opportunity. I stuffed a quarter of the banana into the mouths of Mike and each of the girls and ate the remaining fourth myself. As for the peel, the last telling bit of evidence, I would keep it front and center, and when the customs officer said, "Do you have any—" I would immediately cut him off and proclaim, "I have a banana peel," so as not to be seen as hiding anything. This happened as I'd imagined, and the customs officers smiled at my extreme willingness to comply and directed me to a trash can where I could dispose of it.

"Do you have any alcohol?" the officer asked Mike.

"I don't know," Mike lied. Then he turned to me and asked,

"Do we have any alcohol?" He knew full well that we had half a bottle of vodka in the trunk of the car but apparently wanted me to be responsible for any repercussions. I could almost hear him saying, "Gosh, Officer, I had no idea she'd smuggled that booze in. Obviously she has a problem." I also knew, from scouring the ferry rules, that we were permitted to bring alcohol aboard as long as it stayed locked in the vehicle. They wanted to make sure passengers patronized the ferry bars as much as possible.

"Yes," I said, "we have half a bottle of vodka in the trunk. I'm pretty sure you know that," I muttered.

"That's fine," the officer said. "Just keep it in the car. We'll need you to open the boot," the officer said to Mike. He exited the vehicle, and the two of them proceeded to examine the contents of the trunk of our car. After a moment, other customs officers swarmed to our vehicle. The girls dozed in the backseat. And I waited. And waited. I couldn't imagine what the problem was. Had I forgotten a fruit basket? Did the jelly jar count as fruit?

Eventually Mike returned to the driver's seat.

"Everything okay?" I asked.

"Yeah," he said. "It was the seashells."

Everywhere we went, we found seashells more impressive, unique, and intricate than the previous beach, and I'd amassed a substantial collection along the way.

"They don't want us taking seashells?"

"They just couldn't understand why we'd have them," Mike said. "They kept asking what they were for. Eventually I told them it was for a school project, and then suddenly they were okay with it."

Even though Tasmania is part of Australia, it is also its own, disease-free island where agriculture makes up much of the industry. The customs process is taken seriously. Their restricted-items list gets very specific, including Mexican walking fish, yabbies (a type of crayfish), peas in the pod, and fox urine. I'm not sure how often people attempt to travel with fox urine, but hopefully they're not headed to Tasmania. The myriad restrictions are the Tasmanian government's effort to keep things like didymo (a freshwater algae affectionately known as rock snot), goldfish ulcer disease, and the pea weevil at bay. The close inspection of our seashells was likely to ensure that we weren't at risk for introducing abalone viral ganglioneuritis to Tasmanian waters. Tasmania produces a quarter of the world's abalone harvest, so they're pretty set on keeping the abalone population in good health.

When it was determined we wouldn't wreck Tasmania's ecosystem or economy, we were waved through to a new line where the cars checked in at a little booth. This was where they'd ask to see the vehicle's registration, and I'd have nothing to show them.

"G'day," said a smiling woman peering into the car. "Four of you then?"

"Yes," I said, and leaned across Mike to hand her our reservation. She took a moment to rifle through papers, then handed us a brochure, inside of which were our tickets as well as the key card to our cabin. "Just one more moment," she said, and this was when I was sure we'd be denied further passage, perhaps even arrested on suspicion of vehicle theft. But the registration never came up, and instead she passed us two small tote bags for the children, filled with puzzles and activity books and other memorabilia of the *Spirit of Tasmania*.

Car registration, I would later learn, referred only to the license plate. Additional documentation isn't necessary, and

I'd had nothing to worry about from the start.

The sheer logistics of the vessel, boarding hundreds of vehicles and passengers, were astounding. We drove up ramps and down tunnels in the belly of the ship, guides directing us along the way and bringing each vehicle to rest in perfect alignment with the grid of the vehicles around it. In our family of four, we each had a backpack of books in addition to laptops, blankies, and whatever else we might need for the eleven-hour journey.

"Let's go find our cabin first," I suggested.

"Why did you book a cabin?" Mike asked. "I'd understand if we were on the overnight ferry, but since it's the daytime one, I don't think we'll need it. And isn't it a lot more expensive?"

"They didn't have any other option," I said. "Everything else was sold out." This was true for the journey there, but on the journey back, I'd still booked a private cabin even though cheaper passage was available without one. I was willing to add an extra few hundred dollars to our debt so that we might have a private place to retreat. It seemed too long a journey to do otherwise. And as we walked through the decks of the ship, I was glad for the decision. Passengers sprawled in different places, already staking out their spots, and despite the signs asking people not to lay down and make a bed of the public areas, I could tell that's exactly what they'd be doing.

"We need to get to deck ten," I said.

"Here's an elevator," Emilia said, and she, Ivy, and I approached the elevator.

"We don't take elevators on ships," Mike said. I thought about that for a moment and decided that I agreed. Being stuck in an elevator is disconcerting. Being stuck in an elevator on the water, where lifejackets and lifeboats will do you no good in the event of an emergency, is poop-your-pants terrifying. I didn't want my last thought to be, *If only we'd taken the stairs.*

I did my best to suppress my claustrophobia as we entered the cabin, but images of water flooding the halls came to mind. The girls immediately claimed the two upper bunks and began inspecting their swag. It was ten thirty in the morning, but the stress and scramble of trying to board on time was exhausting. Mike and I crawled onto a lower bunk together, the instinct of a long-married couple, but one quickly thwarted by the narrow bunk. Discomfort trumped the inclination to snuggle. After three minutes, I moved to my own bunk across from him.

After a brief rest, we ventured out to find food and explore the ship. We passed the next ten hours eating, occasionally hitting one of the bars, of which there were many, or snacking on a pie (think mini pot pie, not the dessert variety). We tried to enjoy some of the ship's entertainment. A small movie theater played children's movies, but the ship lurched and rolled, and after only a minute in the theater room, Emilia garnered a greenish hue, and we all went to an outer deck for fresh air. The ship was clean and pleasant, with unimposing stacks of barf bags tucked in every corner, so there was always one close at hand. I'm not often seasick, but the rocking of the ship combined with a slight hangover left me queasy.

When the waters of the Bass Strait calmed and the ship glided smoothly, we watched a presentation on Tasmanian devils and learned more about the disease that was endangering their population, along with Tasmania's considerable efforts to bring the devils back to their full strength in various captivity programs. I already had my sights on a Tasmanian devil sanctuary to visit on the Tasman Peninsula where we could learn more about the animal.

Midday we retreated to the cabin, where Mike, who still wasn't happy about the extra expense, was the first to fall asleep.

"I'm tired too," said Emilia.

"I want to take a rest," Ivy agreed.

So we each crawled into our bunks. Mike's light was already off. I turned mine off. Emilia turned hers off. And then Ivy turned her light off. And suddenly we were entombed in complete darkness. No light bled in from the hallway. I was disoriented within seconds, a discomfort compounded by the rocking of the ship.

"Uh," Emilia said.

"Mom?" Ivy called.

The three of us clawed at the wall to find the light switch. I found mine and turned it on after only a few seconds.

"Phew," said Emilia.

"Yeah," I agreed. "Let's not do that again."

Later, the girls stood in line on deck ten to get their faces painted while Mike drank a beer and I had a glass of wine. The ship began to stir as we reached sight of land, and we returned to the cabin to gather our things. An announcement over the ship's intercom told us to return to our vehicles, and we did so.

The disembarking process was as logistically intricate as the boarding, and I was impressed with the entire scale of the operation. We were told to leave our ignition off until the car in front of us moved, to avoid having hundreds of people sitting in a giant cloud of exhaust fumes. When our lane began to move, the driver in front of us turned the key to his ignition and found he had a dead battery. From just the movement of the back of his head I could see the anxiety and panic that sets in when you realize you are holding up hundreds of people, but there is nothing you can do about it. Eventually, we pulled out around him, and the rest of us moved on, feeling sorry for the guy but also smugly glad that it wasn't us. Ship staff were used to such occurrences and made preparations to jump-start the car.

In Devonport, we checked in to a small cabin at a caravan park, and I was thankful that for the first time we were cabin guests and not campers.

"This place is huge!" Emilia said.

"Look at all this space!" Ivy stretched her arms out wide and twirled around.

"We have a couch!" I agreed.

"And a coffee table!" Mike added.

In truth, the cabin was minuscule but felt downright expansive after the camper. We headed to a nearby grocery store, small and charming, and picked up a variety of goods, including Mike's addition of a pack of creepy sausages, to which he was inexplicably drawn. We didn't get food for dinner, deciding instead to go deeper into downtown and find an actual restaurant. When we did so, we realized that it was late on Sunday evening, and for the most part, the town had shut down. I saw a Subway and a McDonald's and made a silent vow to myself that I would not allow any of my family to eat at or even suggest one of these places. We'd traveled to the other side of the world, crossed a large body of water on an eleven-hour ferry journey, and made it to Tasmania. Under no circumstances would anyone be purchasing a Big Mac. In the end, we bought food to go from a Noodle House. I realize that this too is a chain, but it seemed the lesser of evils. Back at the cabin, I made cocktails for Mike and me, and we ate noodles and tucked the girls into bunk beds. Then Mike and I went to bed, on a real mattress with lots of pillows, and for the first time in weeks, we had our own bedroom door to close.

* * *

Can I Get a Witness?

Please notice what would result from the war in heaven. In his fury,
Satan would bring woe or trouble, upon those on earth. As you will see,
we are now living in that time of woe. But it will be relatively brief—
only "a short period of time." Even Satan realizes that.

—www.JW.org

It was early December, and without any idea what type of commercial or retail options there would be in the semirural areas of Tasmania, Mike felt it imperative to go on a Christmas reconnaissance mission before we left Devonport. The holidays were almost upon us, and no matter how much we'd enjoyed our travels thus far, we knew that if Santa didn't visit on Christmas Eve, our daughters would remember nothing else.

"I think we should get Emilia a skateboard," Mike said. In Byron Bay, she'd become enamored with the skateboard belonging to our hippie neighbors.

"Isn't that going to be kind of a pain in the ass to take back on the plane?"

"Well, I'll just go check it out," he said.

While Mike headed into town, I busied myself once again packing up our belongings and taking a long, glorious shower by myself while the girls jumped on a large jump pillow provided by the caravan park. A jump pillow is one of those things that previous generations view with great envy, because it is so much cooler than the trampolines upon which we injured ourselves as children.

When I'd showered and packed, Mike still hadn't returned, so I set to cooking breakfast for everyone with the plan that he would return, we'd quickly eat, then load up the car and head south. I made eggs along with Mike's beloved creepy sausages. A hot breakfast was somewhat of a treat after our weeks in the camper, where morning meals were never more complicated than toast, which in itself had tasted like luxury.

When Mike returned, we had only a few minutes before checkout time, so I shoved the eggs and creepy sausages at him and hurriedly packed the car.

"So, did you find anything?" I asked on one of my trips to retrieve more luggage.

"Yeah," he said, "it's all taken care of."

"What do you mean? You bought her a skateboard?"

"Yes."

"So we just need to get something for Ivy?"

"I bought Ivy a scooter."

"We now have a skateboard and a scooter to take back with us on the plane?"

"It'll be fine."

"Okay." I was skeptical. "So maybe we should get some stockings and call it good?"

"No," he said. "I got those too. I got *everything*."

For the first time, I knew what Mike must have felt at every past holiday during which I'd handled all of the presents myself. While it's nice to have your spouse take care of the logistics of gifts, you can't help but feel a false, hollow sense when you are as surprised as your child is when she unwraps a gift you ostensibly gave her.

As we drove south from Devonport, the small city faded, and the landscape gave way to farmland with the occasional accompaniment of the smell of manure. Even in Tasmania, signs everywhere warned us that if we were sleepy, we would surely die. But the road was open, the day was beautiful, and a mountain range flanked us to the right. Mike picked up speed on the highway, where the speed limit was 110 kilometers per hour (equivalent to 68 mph). But as soon as he passed 100 kph, the car began a high-pitched beeping, as if warning us to slow down.

"What is that?" Mike asked. "Is there any way to turn it off?"

"I don't know," I said. "But annoying is what that is."

He'd slow down, we'd forget about the annoyance, but then he'd creep back up, and as soon as the speedometer hit 100, the car would once again berate us, made doubly annoying by the fact that we were still 10 kph under the posted speed limit.

We'd driven for some time, and the girls were bored and restless, so we pulled over at a small café called the Perth Road House to get out, stretch, and possibly employ our last resort when traveling of setting up some sort of movie for the girls to watch, as we still had a few hours of driving ahead of us.

We parked, and Mike said, "I'll see if I can't set up a movie on the iPad or something." At home, our children are not permitted to play on iPads or other such devices. We also try to avoid having them do so when traveling, saving it for occasions like this one, when they are truly road weary but we still have hours ahead of us.

"Hey, girls, come look at these birds," I said.

Emilia and Ivy stood with me at a fence that separated the parking lot from a field edged with giant pine trees. A dozen black macaws with yellow accent feathers feasted on pinecones, both in the trees and on the ground. I could have stared at the birds for hours, but Ivy then announced, "I have to poop," and there isn't any possible answer to that other than, "Okay, let's go to the bathroom."

We used the road house facilities, and when we exited, Emilia asked, "Mom, can we maybe get a treat or something?"

"I have granola bars, water, apples, and bananas in the car. That's plenty of food. We don't need to buy something every time we go somewhere."

"Oh, man," she said.

Mike exited the road house, approached us, and said, "Should we maybe get them a treat?"

I felt unintentionally undermined but repeated my justification. "We have granola bars, water, apples, and bananas. And I just told them that we don't need to buy something every time we go somewhere."

"Oh." He looked sullen and scolded. "Okay."

We never did get the movie working, and I felt like the bad guy as we took to the road again, so I broke out a secret stash of cookies for my own redemption as much as my kids' pleasure.

Further south through Tasmania, we passed old buildings and churches, and black cutouts of random people and animals, a soldier, an emu, a dingo. In Jericho, stones placed in the hillside read: Commandant's Cottage 1842. The cottage sits next to the Probation Station, where a few hundred convicts were housed by night, so that they might construct the Old Jericho Road by day. We passed the Forestier State

Forest, and I wondered what makes one forest forestier than another forest. More trees per square kilometer?

After hours of travel, we arrived in the small town of White Beach and located the house we'd booked. As we pulled into the driveway, I said, "Oh yeah, it has a tennis court. I totally forgot about that."

"Are you serious?" Mike asked.

"Yeah. See that?" I motioned to a crumbling court, fenced in and with occasional weeds sprouting through where they could. "That court goes along with this rental."

"That's awesome," he said.

We exited the car, and I used a code I'd been given when making the reservation to gain entry to the single-level but spacious home. It was dated and rough around the edges but, once again, felt like pure decadence after weeks in a camper.

"I can't believe it has a tennis court," he said. "And look, the water is right there." The home faced the water and a sliver of beach, with just one narrow street in between. I was happy that Mike was happy with the home, as this was one part of the trip that I'd booked entirely on my own. We unpacked and settled in, but Mike's initial delight gave way to an edgy panic. "Amanda," he said, "I can't find any information about how to get on the Internet. Did they give you instructions?"

"Uh. I don't think this place has Internet."

"Are you kidding? You booked us a place without Internet?"

"I'm pretty sure I mentioned this before," I said, completely unsure if I'd mentioned it before, though we had discussed the possibility that in the more rural areas, we might have to rely solely on Internet access through the expensive but reliable modem Mike had purchased weeks before on the Sunshine Coast, for such predicaments.

"I'm pretty sure I wouldn't have let you book us a place with no Internet."

I decided to go silent and make myself busy unpacking until the internal meltdown Mike was experiencing ran its full course.

"Mom, come look at this," Ivy called.

I followed the sound of her voice to an enormous bedroom that was home to both bunk beds and a large king-sized bed.

"They have bunk beds!" she exclaimed.

"That's awesome!"

"And there's this big bed right here," she motioned to the king-sized bed, "where you and Daddy can sleep!"

Less awesome, I thought. "Actually, Ivy, I think Dad and I are going to sleep in the other bedroom."

"Aw, man," she said. My daughters do not understand privacy, why anyone would want it, or why I wouldn't want to spend every second of every day with them.

Black swans glided through the waters of White Beach, and small birds with a shock of blue on their backs hopped around on the front lawn. "Look at that little bird, Mama! I'm going to name him Jump Blue," Emilia declared.

We explored White Beach, making special note of where the grocery store and liquor store were. At the grocery store, we bought a few items. I was eager to work more vegetables back into our diet, but the produce was shockingly expensive. We checked out with a few items, and the cashier, a pleasant young girl of about seventeen, asked, "Do you want a docket?"

"Uh . . ." I knew the word, it wasn't entirely foreign, but it took me a moment to translate it into my usual vocabulary. "Oh! A receipt!"

"Yeah." She smiled and giggled nervously.

"No thanks, I'm good."

As we headed back to our Internet-free but tennis-court-accompanied accommodations, Mike spotted a sign for a vegetable stand. "Do you want to go check that out?"

"Yeah. Why not?"

We drove down a dirt road and came to a small building, one end of which was open and provided access to a large refrigerator with four glass doors. Inside were shelves of fruits and vegetables, bagged and priced at approximately half of what they would have cost at the grocery store.

"This is awesome," I said.

"Agreed," said Mike, and we filled our arms with fruits and veggies of all sorts.

"Okay, that should do it," I said. "Now where do we pay?"

"I think right there." Mike motioned to a large locked container with a slit at the top. A sign pointing down to it instructed us to "Please Pay Here."

We tallied up our bill, and I retrieved the money and dropped it in the box. There's a definite joy when you find that somewhere in the world, the honor system is still in use. Its continued use is that reassuring indication that honor still exists.

As we settled into life in rural White Beach and prepared for Christmas by hanging our lone ornament, a stained-glass Christmas bell that a stranger at the campsite in Huskisson had given us, from the living room light fixture, Emilia approached me.

"Mom?"

"Yes?"

"There's something wrong with my face."

"What?" I turned to look, and she indicated her left cheek, in the middle of which nestled a tiny blemish.

"That's just a little pimple, honey. It's nothing to worry about." I refrained from telling her that if she turned out anything like me, she had years of far worse skin to look forward to.

Over the next week, she repeatedly asked me to look at her "nipple." This included loud questions in crowded public places such as, "Is the nipple still on my face?" "When is my nipple going to go away?" "My nipple hurts," and "Mom, will you take a look at my nipple?"

* * *

I loved the cooler weather of Tasmania, but we still had many sunny days when Mike insisted we all trek down to the beach. I'd mistakenly thought that by traveling as far south in Australia as we could, I could get out of any more beach days. But we were always near a beautiful beach, the weather was almost always conducive, and I was forced to admit that at times it can be near pleasant, in a sand-up-your-ass kind of way.

I could escape going to the beach (or work the sand out of my ass if we'd been to the beach) by suggesting we all play tennis on the dilapidated court. The home had rackets and balls and a key to the court. We were the only ones with access, so we took advantage of it. First we'd play with the girls, which sometimes felt like throwing a tennis ball in the direction of their rackets and hoping like hell that some sort of contact was made, because too many misses in a row brought on sullen countenance with tears sure to follow. Eventually they'd grow bored of tennis and play something else, leaving Mike and me to play. I'd never played tennis before. I don't know the rules or how to keep score, so perhaps I use that term too lightly. But we spent a good hour attempting to keep a volley going and laughed along the way.

Later that afternoon, we piled in the car to drive just a few blocks to where we'd seen an information kiosk. The girls picked flowers nearby while Mike and I read about the community and learned the location of the library, not because we were interested in borrowing reading material, but because they offered free Internet at certain times, and Mike was still bitter about my having booked us a place without Wi-Fi. Eventually he would get over this, and we never made it to the library, as it was closed for most of our stay in White Beach due to the Christmas and New Year holidays. Internet through his phone may have been expensive, but it was cheaper than him missing out on work entirely.

We lingered at the kiosk because the girls seemed to be engrossed in a game involving pretending to be flowers, which I enjoyed, because it was a rather quiet game. A sedan pulled up to the kiosk, and after a moment, a man emerged from the driver's seat. Another man sat in the passenger seat but made no move to exit the vehicle.

"G'day," he called.

"Hello," we chimed.

"Are you new to the area? Looking for information?"

"Yes," Mike said. "We're just here for a little bit and thought we'd check it out."

Much of Australian culture thus far seemed very similar to American culture, including standards of dress. This man was dressed just a little too nicely, in what I silently thought of as church clothes. And for a moment I couldn't decide if his overt friendliness was because Australians, by and large, are an inherently friendly people, or if there was evangelism waiting for us at the end of this conversation. I decided he was just plain friendly, as he told us all about the surrounding area, caves to check out, where to see the best wildlife, and indeed, how to interact with it.

"If you see an echidna, they're marvelous creatures. And they'll roll up into a ball if you startle them. But you can actually then pick them up. You do it very carefully. Their quills can draw blood, but if you put one hand like this and the other like this," he pantomimed a delicate scooping up of an imaginary echidna, "you can actually hold them, and if they open up, you can rub their bellies." I was both suspicious and excited, because as much as I know interacting with wildlife is not wise, at that moment I wanted nothing more than to rub an echidna's belly.

I daydreamed of doing so, and when I again tuned into the conversation, the man was telling Mike about his friend in the car. "Bob only has one leg, so it's a bit difficult for him to get in and out of the car. But do you like to read?"

"Uh, sure," Mike said, and I shot him a sidelong glance because we both knew the pitch was coming.

"Hold on just a moment." He returned to the vehicle and retrieved standard Jehovah's Witness reading material. I suddenly remembered we'd passed more than a few street signs that included additional directions to the nearest Kingdom Hall. "The Bible is really interesting. I mean, I find it interesting. I don't know if it's something you study or what it is *you* believe." He stopped there, leaving the prompt to hang in the air while Mike formulated an answer.

"Yeah," said Mike, "you know, we're not really looking to make a change at this time." I tried to hide my smile, because he sounded like he was talking to a cable company rep or cell phone provider, though this man was selling a different type of product.

"Okay then. Well, I'll just leave you with that." He smiled, returned to his one-legged passenger, and went on his way.

* * *

That night, after the girls were asleep, Mike and I covertly brought all of the Christmas gifts into the house and hid them in the closet in the master bedroom.

"Holy crap, Mike. This is substantial." Not only was it a skateboard but a longboard. And for Ivy, he'd purchased a full scooter. Sure, it was collapsible, but these were still fairly large items and a fair amount of weight. He'd also purchased stockings, and I smiled when I saw that he'd purchased four instead of two. Another bag held stocking stuffers for the kids.

"Yeah, I know, but I think they'll really like them."

"Yes," I recanted. "You did really good. Santa's not skimping on Tasmania."

* * *

Port Arthur

The accepted wisdom of the upper and ruling classes in 18th century England was that criminals were inherently defective.
Thus, they could not be rehabilitated and simply required separation from the genetically pure and law-abiding citizens. Accordingly, lawbreakers had to be either killed or exiled, since prisons were too expensive. With the American victory in the Revolutionary War, transgressors could no longer be shipped off across the Atlantic, and the English looked for a colony in the other direction.

—www.History.com

There seemed no better family activity on Christmas Eve than to visit Port Arthur, the infamous penal colony in southern Tasmania. In my fascination with facilities of incarceration, I sometimes forget that many people view prisons in a different and much darker light.

"Come on, girls. Hurry up and eat your breakfast," I said, eager to get going.

"Why do we have to hurry?" Emilia asked.

"Because we need to start our schoolwork?" Ivy guessed.

"No, there's no school today, because instead we're going to prison!" A momentary flash of panic crossed Emilia's face, and I quickly elaborated. "It's not a prison anymore, but it used to be. Now it's like a museum, and we're going to visit it and learn about its history."

"I love museums," Emilia declared.

"Will they have snacks?" Ivy asked.

"Yes, Ivy, they will have snacks. Mike," I called to the living room where my husband worked on his laptop, "your breakfast is ready."

He entered the home's odd little eating room a minute later. "Whoa," he said when he looked at the plate I had ready for him. There were two eggs and an abundance of the creepy little sausages he seemed to insist on always buying. "Please don't make me eat all of that."

"I thought you liked them." In truth, I'd cooked them all simply because I wanted to be done with them. I wanted them consumed or discarded, but one way or the other, I didn't want to have to look at them anymore.

"They're actually kind of gross," he admitted, and I felt a small triumph that he'd finally come to my side of the sausage issue.

It was less than fifteen minutes in the car to reach Port Arthur, the sprawling settlement of more than thirty buildings and ruins that served as a dockyard, timber camp, and most notably, a penal colony. We entered the main building, a mass of intimidating stone, to purchase our admission for the day.

"Well, maybe we should get the two-year family pass," Mike suggested.

"Mike, we don't live in Australia," I reminded him.

"Yeah, but you just never know when we might want to come back." Given how long it would take us to pay off the airfare and campervan, which still occupied large chunks of our credit card bill, this seemed unlikely. "Oh, and let's do that too." He indicated an optional tour of the boys' prison.

"Oh yes," I agreed. "That sounds right up my alley."

"A two-year family pass and four tickets for the boys' prison tour?" the clerk asked.

"Yes, that's correct," I said, though I still could not comprehend a follow-up visit to Tasmania in the next two years. It was somehow endearing that Mike could. I paid, and she handed us a stack of tickets and maps. We each received a playing card as well. "What's this for?"

"At the end of the tour, you'll be able to match your card up with an actual inmate and learn their history."

"This is so cool," I whispered to Mike.

The clerk also handed us two small activity books for the children. I wondered how they might make the information kid-friendly, but when I glanced through the booklet and saw a photograph of a miserable twelve-year-old boy sentenced for stealing, and the question "How would you feel, after four months at sea, arriving in Tasmania?" I decided that a kid-friendly version of Port Arthur wasn't possible.

The grounds of Port Arthur are expansive and contain the ruins of what once was its own community. In addition to the block of prison cells, there were buildings where the warden, guards, and their families lived, a church, an asylum, other miscellaneous structures, and a memorial to the victims of the Port Arthur massacre in 1996. Visitors roam these grounds freely, but a short introduction by one of the facility's tour guides seemed an appropriate start to the day.

We stood on a large green lawn in the sunshine while a guide introduced us to all that we might see on the grounds. He told us about some of the more famous stories of convicts. George "Billy" Hunt was one of these. A convict who attempted escape after finding a deceased kangaroo. He figured it was worth a shot to drape the rotting animal over himself, then hop his way to freedom. But food was apparently not plentiful at Port Arthur during its operation, so two of the guards, spotting this slow and not very agile kangaroo, took aim and prepared to shoot it for a meal. Hunt saw this and threw up his arms in surrender.

The tour guide warned us that while much of the history we'd learn at Port Arthur would inspire sympathy for the inmates, many stories had been romanticized over the years.

"You'll hear stories of a young man imprisoned for seven years for stealing a length of rope. What you don't hear is that there happened to be a prize-winning horse at the end of that rope."

Port Arthur legends, like any, change in the telling and retelling over time. One can't help but wonder which are embellished for greater entertainment value, or in the case of the rope thief, made more dramatic by the omission of certain details. Other stories are likely forgotten altogether or never recorded in the first place, and we are reminded that the intersection of history and truth and fiction is a giant, muddled mess.

The girls fidgeted and sat down in the grass to enjoy the sunshine while we listened intently about the prison's early attempts to blight the moral stain of its prisoners. Church was compulsory for everyone, both prisoners and guards alike, but curtains were put up as shields, so that the pious and decent folk might avoid looking upon the moral stain of the inmates.

All the talk of moral stain made me question my personal level of tarnish. I'm far from pious and spent the bulk of my teens and twenties in a general state of self-centeredness and being an asshole to those around me. And yet, when considering the issue of morality, I decided that my degree of stain was not so great as to be beyond repair. I've never robbed a bank or stabbed someone or worn pajama pants to the grocery store.

The church services at Port Arthur were multi-faith for some time, until a particular Irish clergyman took his post there and, in the course of a sermon, declared that all Catholics would burn in hell. After that, Catholics refused to attend, even the prisoners, and a separate Catholic church was built so that the religious might condemn one another in peace and from afar.

Other famous Irishmen at Port Arthur included political prisoners who were housed separately at William Smith O'Brien's cottage, named for an Irish nationalist who was also a living illustration of why one should never give up hope. Convicted of sedition for his part in a rebellion, he was sentenced to be hanged, drawn, and quartered. That sentence was commuted to deportation to Tasmania to serve a life sentence. After five years, he was released on the condition that he not return to Ireland. Two years after that, he was pardoned and returned to Ireland where he lived the rest of his life. I'm not saying his years of incarceration were easy, and they included a failed escape attempt from Maria Island before being sent to Port Arthur, but it's a long way from being hanged, drawn, and quartered.

Flogging was the punishment of choice until 1848 when the authorities admitted that it didn't actually work. Instead of inmates behaving in fear of the punishment, it became a rite of passage, and a prisoner's ability to withstand a flogging without crying out determined the pecking order within prison society. An alternative punishment was developed by James Boyd, who introduced solitary confinement as a weapon. The separate prison was formed, where prisoners were not allowed to speak with or view another human. If they were led from their cells to another location, they were hooded. This denied them any contact or social interaction. If they misbehaved in the separate prison, the solitary confinement was taken a step further, and they were placed in the punishment cell or dumb cell, a room behind four steel doors, to which no light or sound reached. The guide suggested we check out the room and dared us to spend thirty seconds inside. I decided I would.

But solitary confinement would have to wait, as Ivy tugged at my coat. "Mom, I'm hungry."

"Did you know the prisoners here used to eat gruel?"

"Is that like a granola bar?"

"Um, no."

"Can I have a granola bar?"

"I don't have any granola bars, but let's go check out the café."

We made our way to the café and ordered hot chocolate, cappuccino, and scones, all of which was above and beyond what you'd expect from the café of a major tourist destination and not how I'd ever expect to dine in prison. I don't know for sure but would guess that incarceration facilities run fairly low on baristas.

We sat under a poster that showed portraits of inmates along with their offenses, ranging from murder, rape, larceny, and bestiality to suspected homosexuality. The fact that the latter was considered an offense was heartbreaking. I like to think that we have progressed since those backward times, but then I take a look at the gross failures of the modern prison system, where we punish drug addicts in the same way that we do mass murderers, and I realize that we've done nothing of the sort.

The prisoner portraits are undeniably an important part of the Port Arthur experience. They show weathered faces, hardened eyes, all in the same prison-issued wool coat and a scarf tied at the neck. The origin of these photographs is in dispute. Port Arthur credits them alternately as "probably taken by Commandant A.H. Boyd" or "photograph attributed to Boyd," an accreditation apparently changed from the original attribution to photographer Thomas J. Nevin, who produced a large number of cartes-de-visite (now we'd call these mug shots) for the Australian police. Nevin's descendants and proponents contend that Boyd was never a photographer and are appalled at the apparent misattribution, which they contend was born and perpetuated in faulty academic research, for such an important collection in history. While I'm no historian, the case for Nevin seems substantial, and the possible misattribution remains another example of history blending with fiction, even when dealing with photographic evidence.

The warm scones with fresh cream made the convicts' pictures and lives and realities not quite real. On the one hand, the passage of time that separates us emotionally from the sadness of long ago is dangerous. When inhumanity and cruelty are no longer fresh in our minds, it's easy for us to repeat them. On the other hand, if we carried with us the weight of all of history's devastation, we'd go insane. There's something to be said for a balance between empathy and self-preservation.

As such, it was Port Arthur's massacre of 1996 that affected me deeper than the horrors of the working penitentiary, because I could identify with the victims of that tragedy, mostly tourists like myself, far more than I could relate to a man shipped to Port Arthur against his will in the 1830s. The events of the 1996 massacre were the horrific result of mental instability combined with semiautomatic weapons, in a rural and previously calm area of the world where law enforcement was neither prepared for nor capable of a quick and effective response. I tried to imagine the terror of open fire at a crowded tourist destination. I looked again at the poster of inmate portraits; my mouth drooped, shoulders slumped, and my heart weighed heavy, threatening to drag me lower, both physically and emotionally. This excursion suddenly seemed terribly depressing and a horrible idea for Christmas Eve. But this is where kids come in handy, and I welcomed the interruption of my thoughts.

"Mom, what's a water bubbler?" Emilia asked.

"A what?" I sat a little straighter and looked at my daughter with gratitude.

"A water bubbler."

"Where did you hear that?" Mike asked.

"Is it food?" Ivy asked.

"That sign, right over there," Emilia pointed to a sign that did indeed say water bubbler, and an arrow pointed to what we foreigners refer to as a drinking fountain.

"Mom, I have to go potty," Ivy said.

"Okay, I'll take you." I handed Mike the brochure I held with our tickets. "This has all of our tickets for the boat ride and the tour of the boys' prison," I said.

"Okay."

"It's important, so don't lose it."

"Okay, but why are you making such a big deal about it?"

"Well, if I die, I want you guys to still be able to take the tour of the boys' prison."

But I did return from the bathroom and once again took charge of our important documents. When we'd fought over every last crumb of scone and drop of cream, and I silently thanked the café for not trying to offer authentic prison food, we made our way to the separate prison. I was eager to get into the solitary confinement cell, because I've always been sort of creepy like that. The guide wasn't kidding when he said that the cell was located behind four heavy steel doors, and in between each door was a turn in a hallway, so that light had no means of filtering in when the doors were closed.

"Okay, girls," said Mike. "Step back. Mom wants to get locked in the cell."

"Why, Mama?" Emilia asked.

"I don't know. I guess I just want to see what it's like."

"Okay, but don't be scared," she assured me. "I'll be right here."

I wanted to stay in the cell for thirty seconds, as the guard had suggested, but I also knew that when prisoners were punished in this manner, they might stay in the cell for up to thirty days. The solitary prison was bad enough, and I wondered what it would do to a human to deprive him of interaction. This took it a step further and removed light and orientation with surroundings. It was complete deprivation.

"Go ahead," I told Mike. And he slowly shut the door.

* * *

Have a Solitary Christmas

Solitary confinement is too terrible a punishment to inflict on any human being, no matter what his crime. Hardened criminals in the men's prisons, it is said, often beg for the lash instead.

—Emmeline Pankhurst

I knew that the deprivation cell would be ominous, but until you experience it, it's hard to fully comprehend the impact. The door closed, and I counted to one. One second, and I questioned the concepts of up and down. The floor tilted beneath me. Two. How far away was the wall? Should I put my hand out in front of me to find it? Or should I stay still, afraid that if I moved I would inadvertently smack my skull against stone and die a senseless death, within a prison cell where I was not a prisoner? Within five seconds, I'd already lost any sense of space. I couldn't have found the door, was afraid even to reach out in search of it. I was surrounded by cold stone and darkness blacker than any night I've known. The full cruelty of such a punishment, and the madness that would surely result, hit me. And I think that any proponent of solitary confinement should have to spend a night or two in the box himself.

"Okay, open the door," I said, and the level of panic in my voice surprised me. We were a century and a half past when this cell had been used. We were at a historical site and tourist attraction. My husband, who is an inherently kind person and one who knows better than to play mean pranks on me, stood just on the other side of the door. All of these things should have been reassurances, but I still panicked. What if an earthquake hit during my thirty seconds inside? What if the door wouldn't open?

"How was it?" Mike asked, and I quickly darted past him and away from the door.

"That's inhumane," I whispered. And for the first time, my long-held fascination with facilities of incarceration seemed to me a terrible weakness in my character. I took a few breaths and calmed myself. "Let's get outside in the open air and do something fun," I suggested.

"Okay," Mike agreed. "Do you want to go to the boys' prison?"

"Perfect."

We walked through the ironically beautiful prison grounds to the dock.

"My feet hurt," Ivy said. "And I'm hungry."

We knew by that point that we were short on time. Our girls were fading in both enthusiasm and energy.

"We're going to take a boat ride!" Mike cheered.

"Okay," Emilia said, though her shoulders slumped.

Along the boat ride out to the boys' prison, the tour guide pointed out the Isle of the Dead, a small, adjacent island jutting out of the water. Port Arthur was a fully functioning community and therefore needed a place to dispose of the dead, be they staff and guards or prisoners, though the latter were not given marked graves. Of the more than sixteen hundred graves on the Isle of the Dead, only 180 are marked.

The boys' prison had been located on Point Puer, though it operated for only fifteen years. The site contains very few remains of the actual buildings, but the passion of our tour guide, who obviously lived and breathed his job, painted a very clear picture of what life had been. History books claim that boys transported to Point Puer were as young as nine years old, but our guide assured us that his research detailed a convict of just seven years of age. He informed us that at that time in Britain, a child could work by the age of six and could be hanged for his crimes by the age of seven.

"Girls," Mike whispered. On the short boat ride, which held a tiny counter with drinks and snacks for purchase, he'd bought a package of peanut M&Ms, with the intention of doling them out as bite-sized little bribes for patience and good behavior. He used these to get us through the half-hour tour.

"I don't like the peanut ones," Emilia whispered back.

"Just take it," Mike commanded. "They're good."

"It's very rare that people come up with good ideas in Tasmania," said the guard. Most of the crowd laughed, but as a visitor to this island, I didn't feel entitled to judge it. "But teaching boys skills and separating them from adult criminals was probably a good idea." I agreed that keeping young boys in proximity to the adult inmates could have been disastrous on many levels. But the guard was careful to warn us that life on Point Puer was still far from ideal.

"And what do you think this might have been used for?" the tour guide asked, making a wide sweeping gesture to the shore of Point Puer and the chilled waters leading out to sea.

"For bathing?" someone suggested.

"Washing clothes?" another ventured.

"The toilet?" a third offered.

"Unfortunately," the guide confirmed, "you are all correct."

The weather was cold. We huddled in our jackets, and I looked at the water with fear. I wouldn't have wanted to go in the water (ever), but especially not then, because it was so painfully cold.

"Jeez," Mike whispered. "This is their summer."

That realization made me groan. As awful as having to use the same frigid waters for both bath and toilet was, we were standing there at the warmest time of the year. What must it have been like during their winter?

During its operation, the prison ended up with far more boys than it had the ability to care for. The boys were not housed in cells but large shelters, if they were lucky enough to find a spot. The guards felt that an assignment to Point Puer was a sentence in itself and that they'd been unfairly given the lowliest of positions. Combining the facility's overcapacity with the disgruntlement of the guards resulted in an odd mix of harsh punishments and an archaic free-for-all. Bullying would have been off the charts, and as our guide explained, a stint at Point Puer could have been horrific or a grand power trip, depending on your popularity and with whom you kept company.

"It's like that creepy boys' island from *Pinocchio* and *Lord of the Flies* all rolled into one," I said. Mike shuddered in response.

One of the most famous inmates was Samuel Holmes, immortalized in fiction as the basis for Charles Dickens's Artful Dodger and sentenced to Point Puer at the age of thirteen for steeling ox tongues and a partridge. We also learned of George Higgins, who experienced the punishment of being chained to a log. Going about your business while chained to a log could not have been easy, but for George it was fatal. While the boys did their morning duties in the sea, he fell, could not right himself, and drowned.

"Mom." Emilia tugged at my sleeve.

"Wait just a minute, honey," I said. "I'm trying to listen."

The guard was talking about raisins, something about the boys picking raisins out of their gruel to trade later.

"Mom," Emilia said again.

The guard detailed boys walking around with balls of raisins in their pockets for a full week, and I couldn't help but whisper a small "Ew."

"Mom."

"What is it, Emilia?"

"I don't want these," she said, opening her palm to display half a dozen peanuts, from which she'd sucked the chocolate and candy shell.

"Ew," I said. "Are those from your M&Ms?"

"Yes."

"Well, I don't want them, either. You'll have to hold on to them until we find a trash can."

On any other day, she might have balked or fought me on the issue, but though she and Ivy had tuned out most of the guide's insights, and much of what they had heard they hadn't understood, they carried themselves with greater reverence than usual. I took this as an implication that they still gleaned an overall sense of sadness for long-dead children and thank-fulness at having the dumb luck of being born into a time, culture, and family that spared them such hardship.

By the time we reached home, having wallowed deeply in the misfortunes of others, we were emotionally and physically exhausted but steeped in gratitude.

"I think we need to escape reality for a little while," I said, mixing Mike and myself each a muscled drink.

"I've got just the thing," he said. *"Star Wars!"* And he proceeded to begin a *Star Wars* marathon. I was a little worried how the kids would handle it, as I distinctly remember feeling traumatized as a child after watching Harrison Ford get bronzed or Mark Hamill dehanded or Carrie Fisher used as Jabba the Hutt's plaything. But Emilia didn't seem fazed, and Ivy was content to watch anything with a princess involved. And when I thought of all the true suffering we'd learned of that day, a fictionalized story of a father cutting off his son's hand didn't seem so bad.

While Mike got the first movie going (or the fourth if you're a purist), I set about making Christmas Eve dinner. Most people think of this particular meal as something special. I picture a large table, beautifully set, with an unfortunate, large, and tasty animal in the center. Around the mass of protein, there are dishes filled with various casseroles and salads. Mashed potatoes are somewhere in the mix, and there's a pie cooling for dessert. This is not what I made. Instead, I went with plan B, which I now fondly think of as the crappiest meal I have ever prepared. And I've served up a lot of crap in my time.

It began with schnitzel, which I'd always thought of as German pasta, only because I consistently confuse the word schnitzel with spaetzle. In reality, a schnitzel is a cutlet, the world over. Basically I had giant chicken nuggets disguised as breaded fillets, out of which I made sandwiches. I'm not sure why it was so horrible, but I felt a unique sort of disgrace feeding my family this awful meal as we sat on the couch watching *Star Wars* under our lone ornament. But no one had to suffer gruel or solitary confinement or bathe in his own waste or be chained to a log, so we were happy.

We made it through *The Empire Strikes Back* and put the girls to bed.

"I think we should stay up a bit longer," Mike suggested. "Give them some time to really be sleeping hard before we do the Santa thing. I don't want to be caught in the act."

"Agreed," I said. "I'll go mix us another drink."

Two hours later, we sat mildly sloshed on the couch after a terrible romantic comedy in which everyone was white and beautiful and self-absorbed and horny.

"Oh shit," I said.

"What?"

"Now we have to be Santa Claus."

"Shit," Mike agreed.

And for the next forty minutes, we drunkenly packed the stockings and arranged the two gifts by the fireplace. We were loud and giggled and filled our own stockings with beer and random items from the house. It is a wonder we didn't get caught, because Santa was running low on stealth.

* * *

Children and Other Devils

We call her the Tasmanian devil. She's everywhere.
She's like a little pit bull.

– Natalie Williams, Australian composer

At five thirty on Christmas morning, Mike nudged me into a consciousness for which I was not ready. The overindulgence of the night before settled in my skull.

"Why are you waking me up so early?" I demanded.

"Because it's Christmas, and I want us to be up before the girls."

He didn't want the girls walking out on their own, seeing the two lone, unwrapped presents, and bursting into tears. If we woke them, however, and ushered them into the living room with our own excitement and wonder, they would likely catch it. My head protested, but I got out of bed.

"Girls," Mike said as we crept into their room. They'd been sleeping soundly, and I wished for another half hour of sleep. "I think Santa came."

They quickly discarded their grogginess and dragged themselves from their beds. We walked with them to the living room.

"Oh my goodness," Mike said.

"Whoa!" I mustered.

And it worked.

"Santa brought me a skateboard!" Emilia declared.

"Santa brought candy!" Ivy added, diving into her stocking.

"And it looks like Santa brought you a scooter, Ivy," Mike added. "Maybe Santa wanted you to have a scooter to practice on while Emilia practices on her skateboard."

Ivy ignored the scooter, which I was secretly hoping to try myself, and focused on the stocking, sugar being her main motivator. We allowed sugar in various forms for breakfast and spent a lazy morning continuing our *Star Wars* marathon. By mid-morning, the fog of the previous night's overindulgence had worn off and we took Santa's gifts out to the tennis court.

Teaching Emilia to skateboard would have been a lot easier if Mike or I had any clue how to do so ourselves. Instead, she was relegated to whatever knowledge she'd gained from our friends in Byron Bay. Ivy was similarly ill prepared for the scooter, and my attempts at instruction were of little help. I found both the skateboard and scooter more difficult than what I'd anticipated. It was one of those unfortunate moments of adulthood when you realize that your youthful pliability is gone, and you're in very real danger of breaking a hip. Breaking an arm or a leg is one thing; breaking a hip carries with it an altogether aged connotation, the full maturity of which I am not quite ready to embrace.

With limited parental instruction, neither of the girls lasted long on their respective new wheels. Still, I was pleased by the fact that there hadn't been any complaint over our lack of Christmas tree or the fact that they'd received only one gift each. We'd been guilty in the past of going overboard on occasion but hadn't seemed to have spoiled them beyond repair.

The girls went back inside to the living room for more sugar and movies, and Mike and I spent an hour on the tennis court, working off our hangovers. It's possible we would have played all day, but one by one I hit the tennis balls into thick bushes, over the high fencing, or into a dilapidated pool next door.

We turned off the television and rallied the children for a chilly walk along the narrow beach across from our temporary home. The name White Beach seemed unimaginative and out of place when compared with the myriad unique and unpronounceable places we'd visited thus far in the land down under. We watched the tiny clams, in Australia known as pipis, burrow into the sand with each wave. A light rain turned us back to the house, and as we approached the front door, Emilia said, "Mom, Jump Blue is back."

"Yes, isn't that cute. Look how it jumps." The bird hopped around the lawn.

"Oh man, I just love that little bird," she added.

"Jump Blue on White Beach," I noted. "Perfect."

"Hey, Mom," Ivy said. "White Beach—white Christmas! It rhymes!"

Conversations like these are too perfect to correct, so I simply said, "It sure does, Ivy. Merry Christmas."

* * *

The day after Christmas in Australia, like in many countries, is Boxing Day, which has nothing to do with donning gloves and punching your opponent in the face. The origin of Boxing Day was a time to present servants and tradesman with a Christmas Box, or gratuity. Since the presence of servants isn't as common as it once was, it is now just another day to take off work, over-imbibe, and in Australia, watch "the cricket," as our friendly, local, bottle shop owner informed us. I'd stocked up on booze in advance of the Christmas holidays, and as she'd tallied my alcohol, she'd confided that she'd be closed on Boxing Day. "I'm gone to watch the cricket," she'd said. "I just love the cricket."

Our knowledge of cricket never grew beyond the simple facts that there are teams and innings, and they bat and bowl, though we'd followed the tragic story of twenty-five-year-old South Australia batsman Phillip Hughes, who'd died a month prior after being struck in the head. Cricket isn't considered a dangerous sport when compared with others, but a cricket ball hit Hughes behind the left ear, and Australia held its breath as he spent two days in a coma before passing away.

We decided to spend our Boxing Day in the company of devils and traveled a short distance to a nearby Tasmanian devil sanctuary. Tasmanian devils are the largest marsupial carnivores, at times adorable and at other times exhibiting appalling behavior. The animals mate for days, copulation taking five days or more, and they're terribly unfaithful. Males are known to keep the females hostage in dens to keep them from straying, or at other times forcing the females to accompany them to get a drink so that another male doesn't pop in for a quickie in his absence. The females have about twenty to forty tiny babies. The first four to make it to the pouch and on a teat are the lucky ones, and the mother eats the others. Conservation efforts on behalf of devils have become crucial in the past twenty years as devil facial tumor disease (DFDT) has wiped out nearly 90 percent of the species. There are only a few contagious cancers in existence, and these affect dogs, Syrian hamsters, soft-shell clams, and Tasmanian devils. DFDT causes large tumors on the devils' faces, which eventually grow big enough to obstruct the animals' vision and/or ability to eat, leaving most to starve to death. Sanctuaries like the one we attended focused on breeding healthy animals in captivity in order to bring the population back. With an animal like the devil, found only in Tasmania, the dangers of extinction had been high. And for a time it was thought that the devil would go the way of the thylacine, or Tasmanian tiger, the last of which died from neglect in a Tasmanian zoo in 1936.

The thylacine resembled a striped dog with a long stiff tail, and the last of the species was locked out of its sheltered quarters and exposed to extreme heat during the day and freezing temperatures at night, a rare Tasmanian weather phenomenon, from which the animal was unable to retreat. This was the final atrocity visited upon what was truly a unique animal, one of only two marsupials of which both the males and females exhibited pouches. The female's pouch was of course to protect the young, while the male's pouch protected its retractable scrotal sack during a run through thick brush.

In the late 1800s, the Tasmanian government offered a bounty on thylacines, and the animal was largely demonized by a photograph circulated that showed a Tasmanian tiger with a chicken in its mouth, branding the animal as a wild killer of poultry and livestock. And while thylacines had been credited with occasional sheep and chicken thievery, the photograph used to perpetrate this reputation was later proved to be a mounted animal posed for the camera, as opposed to a rogue thylacine caught in the act. Eventually, the Tasmanian government reversed its stance, realizing that the tiger's population had been destroyed beyond repair. They declared the thylacine a protected species exactly fifty-nine days before the last thylacine died at the Beaumaris Zoo in Hobart, after being forgotten about and exposed to deadly elements.

As depressing as the plight of the thylacine is, research is currently under way to use material from preserved specimens to clone the animal and restore the species. No such hope exists for bringing back native Tasmanians. The last full-blooded Indigenous Tasmanians died more than a hundred years ago, and while aspects of their culture remain, the people and language are lost.

The loss of the Tasmanian tiger has been a major catalyst to extensive and concerted efforts to care for the Tasmanian devil, lest it be relegated to a similar fate. The devils looked cute when napping, and I couldn't help but see a comparison to children. We watched a demonstration as one of the sanctuary's volunteers, clad in knee-high waders, entered a devil pen and hung a giant, raw chicken leg from a bungee cord. What followed was a horrific display of table manners, again forcing the comparison with children, as the devil used its jaw, the strongest of any mammal and sixteen times as powerful as the jaw of a pit bull, to crunch through meat and bone, not leaving a speck behind. The vicious nature of a dining devil, combined with their piercing screech and pungent odor, are perhaps what led to their being called devils in the first place. Early-nineteenth-century explorers referred to the animals alternately as "Beelzebub's pup" and "Sarcophilus Satanicus" (Satanic Meatlover) and "Diabolus Ursinus" (Ursine Devil).

The staff's reverence for the devil was more than apparent, not only in the care they took with the animals and in educating people about them but also in the presence of the Tasmanian Devil Cemetery, where we paid our respects to tiny wooden headstones with names like "Horror," "Grumpy Bugger," and "Bob."

There were other animals at the sanctuary as well, and we once again had the opportunity to feed kangaroos and wallabies, view unique birds and quolls, and scratch the butt of a koala who likely would have preferred otherwise.

"Do you have any wombats?" I asked a scruffy young employee, unable to disguise the hope in my voice. If they had a wombat, I would take my time to fully appreciate the animal. I wouldn't balk at the presence of fleas or the barrier of metal bars between us. I would commune with the animal. I would hug him and squeeze him and call him George, and he would *love* me.

"No," he said. "No wombats."

On the way back to our home, roadkill was plentiful. The most common casualties were possums, but wallabies, the occasional wombat (sniff), and kangaroos were also present. Giant black ravens scavenged the dead, and I imagined that when the Tasmanian devil population had been at full strength, the roadkill was likely cleaned up efficiently and with no trace of carnage left behind.

We reached White Beach, and I felt we'd successfully navigated the holidays despite our odd accommodations and distance from home, at least in its traditional sense. With the inclusions of prisons and diseased devils, we'd fully exorcised the holiday spirit.

* * *

Adventures in Public Toilets

We call them faerie. We don't believe in them. Our loss.
– Charles de Lint

"Mama, what is this?" Emilia asked.

An old radio, circa 1970, sat in the living room. I doubted it even worked, but it fit in perfectly with the rest of the décor, the home, and even the tennis court, all of which were stuck in a land decades prior.

"It's a radio," I said. "It plays music."

"But it's not in a car," she pointed out.

If there'd been a rotary phone, she'd have approached it with the same befuddlement.

"It probably doesn't work," I said, reaching for the power switch. But the longevity of radios cannot be discounted, which is why they so often present themselves as life-saving instruments of communication in nostalgic media. You always know that when the stranded hero finds an old radio, it will end up saving him.

Small, remote towns have the best and most entertaining of radio stations, and as soon as we turned it on, we found we had Tasman Peninsula radio clearly coming through.

"Bingo on the first Friday of the month," the deejay said. "I think that's today." Pause. "And on *Sunday* the Dunalley Golf Club will have their Sunday dinner. While you're there, check out their *Wednesday* menu. I can't remember the name of the road, but you make a left. There's a sign."

"Wow," I said.

"So awesome," agreed Mike.

Having covered all of the area news, he moved on to weather.

"Sea's one to two meters, but keep in mind that it could be twice what I said. And that's your weather report."

"Girls, we need to do a little bit of schoolwork," I said. Having survived both the camper and the holidays, I felt that reinstituting some sort of school schedule was a priority. I turned the radio down as ABBA's "Gimme! Gimme! Gimme! (A Man After Midnight)" took the place of the vague and limited weather report.

"Yay, school!" Ivy cheered and ran to retrieve her crayons, all that she'd need in the continuation of her kindergarten curriculum.

"Ugh, no, not school! Why do we *always* have to do school?" Emilia whined.

"What do you mean *always*," I countered. "You haven't done any schoolwork in *weeks.*"

"Ugh," she repeated, and dropped her forehead to rest on the dining room table.

Emilia and I slogged through math worksheets and reading comprehension while Ivy traced numbers and letters. On the radio, "Gimme! Gimme! Gimme! (A Man After Midnight)" gave way to "Dancing Queen," followed by "Take a Chance on Me," and I wondered if the deejay had fallen asleep after pushing play on the first ABBA song. But he returned after the three-song set, and I hoped for more news of the Tasman Peninsula. Instead, it was time for a commercial break, which I found as entertaining as the community calendar had been, with ads for a funeral home and a meat-delivery service.

An hour later, it was time for a break. Emilia had surpassed my expectations by completing her assignments without a single meltdown. Both girls had even made journal entries. Ivy's was a drawing of a Honey Nut Cheerio, while Emilia logged: "Santa brought me a skateboard. Mom made me do homework and we are still in Australia."

"Is it time to get out of the house?" Mike asked, shutting his computer, apparently due for a break himself.

"Yes!" Emilia and I answered emphatically and in unison.

"I want to watch a movie," Ivy said.

"Overruled," Mike answered.

Instead we piled in the car and drove to Hobart to visit the Salamanca market, which began as twelve stalls in the early seventies and now numbers more than three hundred. It is famous enough that I anticipated it would be as impressive and amazing as the market in Eumundi (which started in the late seventies with just three stalls), rather than the small step above a flea market that we'd stumbled on in Huskisson.

Hobart, with a population of a few hundred thousand, is one of only two major cities in Tasmania. It serves as a hub for cruise ships and, more interestingly, is the base port for Antarctic activities and expeditions. Launceston is Tasmania's other big city, with a population not too far above one hundred thousand. While I concede that those numbers might not seem major when compared to cities with millions of people, they are substantial when compared with the rest of Tasmania.

The market didn't disappoint but was a bit overwhelming in both size and density of the crowd, and in more than one instance, I held tightly to each child as we navigated narrow pathways through throngs of shoppers. The problem with going to a major market as a family of four is that we have to stay together but are drawn in four different directions. Emilia wanted to look at children's books, Mike wanted a hat, I was interested in Australian jewelry, and Ivy darted toward anything resembling a sequin.

At one end of the hundreds of stalls, the market sloped upward, so that when you reached the pinnacle, you looked back on the snaking rows of canopied merchants, a collage of color against the backdrop of stone buildings. Like Eumundi, I was convinced that if you lived near the Salamanca market, you could find nearly everything you needed to live in just a weekly market trip. Vegetables, clothing, gifts, stationary, books, spices, beauty products, flowers, what more could one possibly need? Perhaps a hardware store, but beyond that, not much.

We walked the length of the market twice, trying to allow everyone an opportunity to ogle their desired wares, before the complaints began of aching feet, thirst, and hunger.

"If we want to make this last a little bit longer," Mike said quietly to me, "there's a silver bullet in that row of shops over there."

I looked to where his eyes darted and saw a sign for the Faerie Shop. This wasn't a stand set up for the market but a permanent shop devoted entirely to the worship of faeries and all things sparkly.

"Wow," I whispered back. "You sure you want to go down that path?"

"Yeah," he answered. "But I might hang by the door. I'm getting panicky just thinking about it."

Mike is not above embracing tutus and princesses, but Hobart's Faerie Shop was definitely over the top. At the entrance, we walked through a corridor so pink and sparkly that even I felt a sense of panic. At the end of the corridor was a small sitting area where children gathered to listen to a staff faerie tell faerie stories. A nearby container graciously invited donations, and I was more than happy to oblige, as my daughters sat rapt. In an adjoining room, one could easily spend a small fortune on faerie wings, dresses, headbands, and all manner of similar accoutrements.

"And do you know," the faerie on duty told the girls, "that if you write a faerie wish on a piece of paper and drop it in the faerie well, it will come true?"

"Oh dear," I muttered.

Emilia promptly elbowed other little girls out of the way and wrestled her way to the faerie well, where she wrote: "I want to fly and breathe underwater. Love, Emilia."

Ivy, less skilled in the art of bullying her way to the front, waited at the back of the line until it was her turn, at which point she stated her wish, and Emilia transcribed it for her: "I want to be a princess. Love, Ivy."

The stop invigorated our daughters enough to continue through one more pass of the market so that Mike and I could purchase a few souvenirs. We were wrapping up our Hobart adventure when Ivy said, "Mom, I have to poop."

"Okay, sweetie," I said. "Let's go find the bathroom."

Mike lingered outside the restrooms while the girls and

I stood in a long line for the women's public toilet. The wait would be significant. And yet there was a large handicapped bathroom that no one was using. I debated going for it but was reluctant. I wasn't sure how Australian protocol handled such things. In the States, people use whatever is available but of course defer to handicapped and the elderly when they are present, but the Aussie crowd seemed to deliberately refrain from doing so, as if this bathroom was for the *exclusive* use of the handicapped. Until a teenage girl took one look at the line in which we stood and instead opted for the handicapped bathroom. As soon as she emerged, I grabbed my girls by the hands, and we went for it too. I reasoned that being *one* person responsible for the bladders and bowels of *three* people should grant me a temporary qualification for the use of such facilities.

Of all the public restrooms we'd used, in campsites, on beaches, even at gas stations along the way, I'd been continually amazed by the level of cleanliness. That wasn't the case in Hobart, likely because the bathroom had been used dozens of times by that point on market day.

And it seems the dirtier the bathroom, the longer my girls want to hang out in it. Both of them took their sweet time moving their bowels in that foul room, and by the time they finished, my skin crawled. We hastily rinsed our hands in the absence of soap. The facility was a large, single stall, and when I attempted to open the immense steel door that ostensibly slid open, I could not. The claustrophobia of the Port Arthur dumb cell returned. The door was heavy and stuck, and the filth of the room threatened to put me in a full-blown panic attack, though my girls seemed happy to spend the rest of the day there. Ivy sat down on the floor, and Emilia ran her hands along the wall.

"Stand up and stop touching things, girls," I barked. "Don't touch *anything.*"

I wrestled with the door for a minute longer until I was able to shift it, half an inch at a time, into an open position. On the other side stood two old ladies waiting to get in. As I wedged the door fully open and we emerged, the old women entered, and I wondered if they'd be able to get themselves out. The spaciousness of a larger bathroom to accommodate various handicaps is less than helpful if it traps the users inside.

On the drive back to the Tasman Peninsula, I heard the girls chatting over who'd made out better. We'd bought each of them a few books from a used bookstand at the market. Their tone grew serious until Emilia projected her voice to me in the passenger seat and said, "Mom, Ivy's bladdering!"

"Oh my god, what?" I could only assume that bladdering meant something to do with a leaky bladder. Was Ivy peeing on the seat? Had I rushed her too much in the bathroom, not allowing her time to finish? "What do you mean she's bladdering?" I craned my neck to the back, but Ivy sat calm and still and apparently dry.

"Oh." Emilia grinned. "I mean she's bragging."

"Well, I'm sure you two can figure it out," Mike said.

As we got closer to White Beach, we drove on a narrow rural road and I saw something up ahead. An echidna crossed the road in a half-lumber, half-waddle.

"Stop the car!" I yelled, and dove out before Mike had reached a full stop.

I approached the echidna and followed along at a distance as it made its way to a burrow. The animal fascinated me. I tried to recall what the Jehovah's Witness had said about picking one up but ultimately decided that interacting with quilled wildlife was not a stellar idea. So I simply watched in awe as the echidna went on its way. It was a beautiful moment until an angry driver blared his horn, upset at us having pulled over in an awkward spot.

"I love echidnas," I said to Mike when I got back in the car.

"I know, honey, but let's try not to cause a car accident."

* * *

Love on the Beach

Gambling: The sure way of getting nothing for something.
—Wilson Mizner

Because we'd waited too long to make our peak-season travel plans, we ended up with an odd itinerary and an eclectic mix of accommodations, which extended beyond our dilapidated but spacious White Beach home. We'd initially planned to stay in the home for the duration of our time in Tasmania, but there were three days in the middle of our stay when it was already booked, forcing us to vacate for a few nights, then return to finish our time in southern Tasmania, before returning north to the ferry in Devonport.

When I located a hotel in Triabunna with availability for the three days of our displacement, I took it. Triabunna was a fun word to say, and I often mistakenly give credence to locations based on how much I enjoy saying the name of the place. It sounded much nicer than Orford, which was near Triabunna, and sounded like the ugly duckling of the two. I know that basing a place's value on the lyric qualities and cadence of its name is irrelevant, but logic doesn't always prevail.

We packed up everything from the White Beach home and began the drive, stopping early at a gas station in Dunalley where a kind couple named Ralph and Marlene, who ran the place, patiently listened as Emilia related her life story, all seven years of it, to them.

We took the Wielangta forest drive, which boasted two-hundred-year-old trees and a safe haven for a handful of species, including the eastern barred bandicoot. When I encounter words like bandicoot, I'm immediately compelled to learn more. It's intriguing and fun to say, much like Triabunna. I didn't glean much knowledge on the bandicoot beyond that it is the size of a rabbit and yet another marsupial, making me wonder just how many pouched species live in Australia. Because I've never been shy about sharing the depths of my ignorance, I admit that I would have guessed a dozen or two. The actual number is upward of two hundred.

We took the forest drive because Mike had looked at a map and thought it might be more fun for us to take a different, more rural path instead of driving along the main highway again. I agreed and looked forward to a little spontaneity, because it meant we could abandon the constant and increasingly annoying consulting of the GPS. We would truly adventure instead of carefully plodding along a previously mapped-out route. But then we came to a crossroads.

A sign told us that we could proceed straight to Thumbs, or turn right and head to Rheban.

"What do you think?" Mike asked me, and to my dismay, he immediately picked up his phone to check the GPS while the car idled.

"Well, that's a no-brainer," I said.

"I agree." Mike nodded. "We take the direction toward the coast." He looked up from his phone and indicated the road that led to the right, to Rheban.

"Are you kidding? We go to Thumbs. There's a place called *Thumbs*. We can't not go there."

"Oh, uh, okay." He put down his phone and headed straight, and I recognized his reaction as indicative of the fact that despite his asking for my opinion, he didn't really want it.

"There's no phone connection out here," he grumbled as we continued on.

"Yay!" I clapped.

Because Australian culture is similar to American culture, we'd mistakenly assumed that there would be Internet everywhere. And if we'd been in major cities, there would have been. But just as a tourist wandering through the wilderness in Wyoming would find no Internet signal, neither did Internet in Tasmania abound.

As we drove toward Thumbs, Mike kept looking to the right, to the road not taken. "This road seems to be leading us away from the coast," he said.

"We don't *always* have to be at the beach," I said.

"Hmm." He seemed to disagree, and after another minute of driving, turned the car around and headed back to the crossroads so that we could instead head to Rheban.

Ten minutes later, we parked at Rheban beach.

"Another beach?" Ivy whined.

"She's right, you know," I said to Mike. "We don't have to stop at every beach we come to."

"Yes, we do," said Mike. "I can't understand why we'd drive by a beach and not check it out."

"I love the beach!" said Emilia.

And of course, because Mike is insufferably right 96 percent of the time, Rheban beach ended up being the most spectacular one of our entire trip. It was a privately owned but publicly accessible beach with a beautiful view of Maria Island, which I remembered hearing about on the ferry ride as a location for disease-free devils, where they might hopefully flourish and strengthen the animal's population. While I rooted for the devils, I also pictured the wombats frolicking happily on Maria Island and feared for their safety.

"Do you want to take a bag for seashells?" Mike asked before we strayed too far from the car.

"No, we have too many seashells as it is. And anyway, I want to keep going to Triabunna," I added.

Ivy and I lagged as Mike and Emilia charged forth to, what I had to admit, was a magnificent landscape. I was constantly torn between the spectacular view and picking up seashells, each more amazing than the last. My hands were full after just a minute.

"Here," Mike said. He'd been wearing two T-shirts. He took off the top one and tied it into a makeshift bag so I could carry all the shells.

"It's going to get all dirty and sandy and wet," I said.

"That's okay."

It was an undeniably romantic gesture. He could have taken a more I-told-you-so attitude about the fact that I'd wanted to visit Thumbs and his instincts had been the right ones to follow. Then again, I later learned that the sign for Thumbs indicated passage to the Three Thumbs State Reserve, location of the Thumbs Lookout, which was apparently well worth the trip. All of this reinforced my growing suspicion that when making a choice of which attraction to visit in Australia, barring a few rare exceptions, any decision would be a good one.

"You're really going to sacrifice your shirt for my ever-growing and unmanageable seashell collection?"

"I sure am."

"I love you," I said. "And not just because you're hot." I emptied my armful of shells into his impromptu receptacle. "But mostly."

He smiled, and we held hands while the girls ran on ahead of us, finding sea stars along the way. I'm not sure when the switch was made, but when I was a child, sea stars were known as starfish. And sure, they're not fish, but changing the name of something like that just makes parents look like idiots, because we use different terminology than what our children are taught in schools.

I was starting to warm up a little bit to beaches, gaining a greater understanding of why people like them so much. There is something romantic and calming and beautiful about this meeting in nature of earth and water. And the Rheban beach was nearly deserted. Much of my disdain for beaches can be attributed to crowds of people and screaming children. But walking along Rheban beach was an experience on a different level.

However, I still didn't understand why anyone would name a drink "Sex on the Beach," because sex on a beach was a horrible thing to consider. It might sound like a good idea at first, but then your mind focuses in on some of the details. A gritty surface underneath, the possibility of being seen, ants, sand fleas, a rogue wave that could bring with it all manner of slimy creatures, the possibility of being arrested, and the general discomfort that comes from combining sand and nudity.

"Mom," Ivy interrupted my thoughts on the impracticality of sex on a beach and ran toward us. "Guess what I found?"

Her excitement led me to believe that when she opened her hand, I would be presented with the most beautiful shell ever and that she might let me have it. Or perhaps a diamond or a pearl or a twenty-dollar bill.

"What is it?" I asked.

"A piece of sand!" She uncurled her fist to reveal . . . sand.

"Wow, Ivy, that's really great." I tried not to sound sarcastic. But failed.

Five minutes later, she again approached with excitement. "Look what I found, Mom." And I looked up see her holding a hermit crab the size of a grapefruit.

"Holy crab!" Mike said, and I could tell he'd barely kept himself from a proclamation of *crap*.

"You should probably put that down, Ivy."

"Okay," she said, placing the crab at the water's edge, "but I'm going to name it Sparkle."

When we finally departed Rheban beach, I had to admit that the place was a bit magical and I was sad to go.

To reach Triabunna, we would first drive through the unfortunately named town of Orford. When we arrived there, I was surprised to see that Orford was a lovely town with restaurants and activity, bordering an inlet that created a busy area of water play for locals and tourists. I figured if Orford was this nice, Triabunna was sure to be spectacular.

We parked in Orford, because there was a beach area, and even after Rheban, Mike hadn't had his fix. We had to get out and check out the beach. We hovered at the back of a group of people watching others frolic in the water with a variety of water toys. We received a few looks from the people on shore, and after a moment, we realized that this was one big family, not a mix of strangers enjoying the beach. A grandmotherly type, grayed, stooped, and friendly, approached us. "How you going?" she asked.

"My name is Emilia, and I'm from America," Emilia said.

"Is that right?"

Emilia's openness fit right in with Australian hospitality most of the time, and this was no exception. Within five minutes, we learned of the woman's life, and she of ours. Emilia detailed our life in the camper van, her experiences with the Australian lorikeets in Huskisson, and the likely goings-on of her second-grade classroom back in the United States.

"I lived in a caravan too," the woman said. "Our house burned down in a brushfire, and we lived in a caravan for ten months while it was rebuilt."

Any complaints I'd made of our two weeks traveling down the coast now cast me in the most selfish and spoiled light.

"Is there anywhere around here to rent paddleboards or rafts or kayaks?" Mike asked.

"Oh, I don't think so," she said. "No, nothing like that here." We looked at the crowds playing in the water and on the beach and realized that they were all either locals or had brought their water toys with them. "But you are more than welcome to use ours," she said, stepping aside and encouraging the rest of her family to do so, providing us a path to their wealth of gear.

"You are too kind, but no thank you," I said, while putting a hand on Emilia's shoulder, as she was ready to climb, fully clothed, into one of their inner tubes. "We're headed to check in to our hotel; we just wanted to stop and look at the beach area."

She smiled and turned back to Emilia. "Do you know this one?" She took hold of Emilia's arm and began singing a nursery rhyme with accompanying arm movements, which involved walking her fingers up Emilia's arm and ended with her tickling Emilia's armpit. Emilia giggled, encouraging the woman for another. Each nursery rhyme ended in Emilia's delight with tickling, and the woman sang four in all. Some were entirely foreign to me, while others were variations of rhymes I'd grown up with, like "Incy Wincy Spider" as opposed to the "Itsy Bitsy" one. Normally I might have balked at a stranger putting her hands on my child in such a manner, but I held out hope that this woman might adopt us.

After there were no more rhymes to be recited or armpits to be tickled, we said our farewells and returned to the car. When we entered the neighboring city of Triabunna, we saw quickly that Orford was the gem of the two.

Our hotel boasted a drive-through bottle shop, for when purchasing alcohol is of such priority that you can't be bothered to park. Our room was a long, narrow space with an unusual layout. We entered into an area with a queen bed and kitchenette, followed by a hallway and bathroom, which separated the front area from the back, where twin beds awaited the children. It was a design that afforded us a greater amount of privacy than what we'd come to expect when sharing a hotel room with our children.

The main source of income for the hotel appeared to be the gambling offered in the hotel bar, as opposed to the renting of rooms. It was a sad example of gambling addictions in play, with people sitting for hours nursing beer while betting on dogs and horses. The Australian government has gone as far as imposing daily limits on how much money one can bet, a policy of good intentions, for sure, but one that seems destined to be as effective as America's war on drugs. Notices regarding resources for obtaining help when one's gambling has gone out of control served as the lobby's decor, and it was fairly clear that we wouldn't be spending too much time hanging out in the hotel lobby with our kids.

We ventured into Triabunna to see what other options were available. The Triabunna marina served as a launch point for tours to Maria Island, and it was apparent that without that activity, there wouldn't have been much more to Triabunna—or any means of sustaining the few local businesses there, the most remarkable of which turned out to be The Fish Van. This wasn't my nickname for the place; it was, in fact, a food truck called The Fish Van operating near the dock. The name, combined with the promise of fried fish served in a paper cone, won me over from the start. I knew I'd found the gem of Triabunna.

* * *

Burn Out

*On Wednesday, the International Fund for Animal Welfare,
which is also helping provide for burned koalas, put out a call
for volunteers to knit mittens, which could be used as paw protectors
for the injured animals. Within one day, reports* Today,
volunteers had pledged more than 500 mittens.

—Ryan Grenoble, *Huffington Post*

The Fish Van turned out to be so good that I wondered if I hadn't judged Triabunna too harshly. Perhaps the tiny town held other hidden gems that I was overlooking. On our first morning there, we drove around the few blocks of town and found a small business that appeared to be, in part, a restaurant. Inside we found a counter where we could order breakfast, along with an odd room dotted in video games, a wall with movies for rent at six Australian dollars a night, and an assortment of products for sale, including Zippo lighters decorated with various pornographic images.

"Classy," I muttered. But the food was more than palatable, and we filled up on breakfast before heading back to the car to spend the day exploring the area. "Ivy," I said, "you're just going to have to bring that with you."

She was nursing an orange juice like it was a martini. And while I certainly don't want my children to inhale their food, Ivy eats incredibly slowly. At one point, I thought that her daycare in the States was withholding lunch, as she would return at the end of the day with the fully packed lunch I'd sent her off with that morning. She'd always tell me that she didn't have time to eat. When I inquired with the teacher, she said that Ivy has forty-five minutes to eat, but she talks the entire time instead. At home, we often sit down to dinner and spend an additional painful hour waiting for Ivy to finish. Emilia and Mike will eventually leave the table to move on to other things. I don't want Ivy sitting by herself, because that seems both callous and sad, so I sit at the table with her as she takes minuscule bites of food. The upside is that she's in no danger of choking.

In the car, I read through a tourist pamphlet as we headed from Triabunna to Swansea.

"I think we're coming up on Spiky Bridge," I said to Mike.

"Why do they call it that?"

"I don't know, but it's a stone bridge built by convicts in 1843."

"So that's why they call it Spiky Bridge," Mike said. I looked up as we passed stone walls flanking a bridge. Its muted shades of brown blended with the earth from which it sprouted, and it might have camouflaged itself entirely, save for the top row of stones, which were inexplicably laid vertically, perpendicular to the horizontal rows of stones underneath. They jutted into the air and could only be described as, well, *spiky*. Rumor has it that these were placed so to keep cows from falling off the bridge. And I wondered if the inclination of cows to climb a three-foot stone wall and plummet off the other side was inherently Tasmanian, as I'd never known cows to be prone to such behavior, though I've never claimed to be an expert on bovine matters.

Leaving Spiky Bridge behind, we continued on our way to Freycinet National Park. This is another puzzling Australian pronunciation, though it might not have been if I'd had any background in French, which I do not. Every time I saw the word, I would say "fray" and then trail off, sometimes returning at the end of the word to add in "inct" so that it would come out like precinct with an F, frecinct. This is entirely incorrect. The correct pronunciation is FRAY-sin-ay. I much preferred calling it Wineglass Bay, which is a specific location within the national park. I really wanted to go there, because again, I'm influenced by names, and somewhat of a wino. How could I not go to Wineglass Bay? But I'd heard it was difficult to get to, and I didn't know if it would happen or not.

"Mom!" Ivy whined from the backseat, interrupting my thoughts. "You made me spill!"

I turned from the passenger seat of the car to look at her in the back. A bump in the road had caused a minuscule amount of orange juice to spill on her dress.

"Excuse me? How did *I* make you spill?" I demanded.

Her face had been near tears, but now, realizing how ridiculous her statement had been, a smile crept in.

"I didn't touch you," I continued. "I'm not even driving. You are holding your orange juice, and yet somehow you immediately decided that this was my fault? How is it my fault? Because I'm your mother? Is that why it's my fault?" She didn't respond but hid an embarrassed smile and waited an entire day before returning to the universal practice of blaming parents for a variety of things that are completely out of our control.

We drove along and saw a sign indicating a turn for Pontypool. Mike immediately followed it.

"Why are we turning down here?" I asked.

"I just want to check it out," Mike said.

"It doesn't look like there's anything there," I protested. After a moment, he agreed and headed back to the main road. "You were hoping for a pool, weren't you?" I asked.

"What are you talking about?"

"You turned down that road because it said Pontypool and you were hoping for water of some sort."

His silence confirmed it.

We spent the next two hours getting out at various beaches to check them out, despite the fact that it was cold and windy and not a great day for the beach. None of this was enjoyable, and all delayed us in reaching Wineglass Bay.

"Mike, the weather sucks. Can we please stop stopping at every beach we pass? No one wants to walk around on a cold, windy beach."

"I can't help it," he said. And I realized he was right. He could no more pass by a beach without checking it out than the patrons of the Triabunna hotel could pass by a gambling slip without placing a bet. Of all the things he could have found irresistible in this world, I decided beaches weren't so bad. We returned to the car and drove on, eventually spotting a sign for Kate's Berry Farm.

"Turn there!" I said. I was sure this was a good idea. We'd pick berries, which was a much better activity in light of the weather. When we pulled into Kate's Berry Farm, we saw that you couldn't actually pick berries. You could go to the café and eat lavender ice cream topped with blackberries or buy expensive products made from Kate's berries, which must have been grown in soil containing flecks of gold, for nothing else explained the prices of that place, except perhaps that it was packed. And if you can get away with charging fancy prices for fancy berries, you will.

"Kate can keep her damn berries," Mike muttered.

"Ooh, Mom, look!" Emilia pointed to a case containing expensive desserts. The price of just one of them would buy dinner for our family of four at my beloved Fish Van.

"Not happening," I said.

Eventually we made our way to Freycinet and to Coles Beach, the one beach that appeared to be sheltered from the inclement weather. The day had been a bust until then, but I'd come to accept that Mike would somehow find a way to make a beach day out of it. We situated ourselves with beach blanket and cooler and an incredible view, and once again I had to admit that if I let Mike follow his instincts, it usually paid off in the end.

"Mom," Ivy said. "I have to poop."

"Of course, sweetie," I said. We'd had about a minute of sitting with our shoes off but reversed these actions and walked back up the path to where we'd parked the car, just a block or so past a boat launch area and small dock. Two single stalls comprised the marina's public men's and women's restrooms, and Ivy and I went into the women's, which was empty, though I could see another family headed in our direction. When she situated herself on the toilet, I could tell from her expression, as any parent can, that we were going to be there for quite some time. The door rattled. "Just a minute," I called. "Ivy, are you done yet?" I knew the answer was no.

"I don't know," she said, feeling the pressure of strangers waiting outside. "I think maybe."

She'd peed but moved in the unmistakable manner of one who needs to poop. We flushed and exited to allow the other people to use the bathroom. When they were finished, we reentered the bathroom for what would be round two of Ivy's bathroom extravaganza.

A quarter of an hour later, we returned to the beach, and I joined Emilia in shin-deep water to look at some of the seashells in the water, conical and beautiful and perhaps worthy of adding to our collection.

"This one looks nice," I said, picking up a shell. As I held it up, the water drained out, reassurance that a sea creature wasn't living inside. "It's so pretty," I said, and then thirty or so sand fleas fled the shell and began crawling on my hand. These were the type of creatures repellant not for their size or jaws but for their sheer speed, much like the fear people have of cockroaches, despite the fact that they will not actually harm you. I screamed and dropped the shell and decided to return to the beach blanket and drink a beer.

As I did so, weighing the probability of a future nightmare in which sand fleas would colonize in my ears, Mike said, "So, do you think you'd ever want to camp down the Baja Peninsula?" And I did the only thing I could: laugh. "Okay, maybe that was a stupid question," he added. I could do nothing but keep laughing. "Okay, I get it," he said. "The answer is obviously no."

We've spent a lot of time in Mexico over the years, and at some point we decided that as much as we love Mexico, we don't want to use our opportunities to travel on one specific place. There is too much of the world to see. Beyond that, if we did return to Mexico, I wouldn't want to travel with our children through some of the more tumultuous areas. But most of all, I hadn't yet recovered from our two weeks in the camper van, and any other mention of any form of camping was just too soon. I finally stopped laughing when I saw a bug crawling on the blanket next to me.

"What is that?" I said. "Oh, there's another one." And as I leaned back and widened my scope of view, I saw that the same tiny creatures who'd emerged from the shell I'd picked up also inhabited the beach and were suddenly determined to make known their dismay with our presence there. "Crap, they're everywhere!"

"They're just little sand fleas," Mike said.

"It's an *infestation*," I screamed, standing up. "I can't take it anymore!"

"Mommy, can we go for a walk?" Emilia asked.

"That's a great idea," Mike said, addressing the girls. "Let's go on an *adventure hike.*" He then turned to me and in a quieter tone said, "Deep breath. Everything is going to be okay."

When we drove back to Triabunna later that day, we again passed Spiky Bridge and handfuls of cyclists. Cycling an entire lap around Tasmania, broken up into small segments, is popular among those proficient on two wheels (I prefer four). One of the legs of the route is Triabunna to Freycinet, which accounted for the moderate bike traffic.

"What is that ahead?" Mike asked.

"It's just another biker."

"No, *that.*"

We slowed as we passed a small fire, though the local firefighters seemed to have it under control. Turning on the radio, to a station slightly more up-to-date than my beloved Tasman Peninsula one, we heard news reports of brushfires raging on the mainland, one of Australia's most difficult environmental issues. Because the land down under contends with issues of fires, drought, and rising temperatures, it has also become a country far more conscious of and attentive to its use of natural resources. In addition to letting you know that if you are tired while driving, you will surely die, billboards in Australia also promote water conservation, and the Australians we encountered truly seemed to care. I was reminded of our Queensland home and the owner's concern for our use of water. I couldn't help but wonder how our consumption compared to others'. I thought I'd been conscientious and hoped that to have been the case, but I suspect that my neurotic tendencies to constantly clean things undermine my good intentions. I frowned with the realization that when it comes down to it, I am not good for the environment.

We finally returned to our hotel, and when I opened the door, I saw that the room had not been cleaned. The plates from our Fish Van dinner were still stacked by the microwave as I'd left them, though thankfully we'd removed the paper that our fish and chips had been wrapped in the night before, lest our room reek like a true chippery. This was disappointing, because to me, the best part of staying in a hotel room is that magic cleaning fairies come and tidy up every day while you're out. I went to the front desk and found that ours was the only room that hadn't been cleaned, and they didn't really know why.

"Can I get a set of clean plates from you?" I asked.

"Of course," replied the desk clerk. She handed me four plates for our kitchenette, which was really a microwave, shelf, plates, cups, and mini-fridge but no sink, so I couldn't wash the plates from the previous night. I balanced my disappointment at having a stack of dirty dishes in our room with the thought of how much water would be saved by my inability to wash them.

Once again, we dined on takeout from The Fish Van. After which I was eager to shower (quickly for efficiency, of course), not yet having shaken the feeling of sand fleas on my skin.

Halfway through the shower, Emilia burst into the bathroom and said, "Mama, there's a fire right next to our hotel!"

"What?" I wondered if I should grab a towel and run from the hotel with a kid under each arm. Where was Mike? Had he already succumbed? Was he gallantly pitching in and living out his long-abandoned dream of being a firefighter? Was a raging fire sweeping across Triabunna to burn us to embers at any second?

"Come see the fire!" Emilia said.

"What's happening?" I demanded as I came out of the bathroom, clad in only a towel and dripping. "Do we need to evacuate?"

"Uh, no," Mike said, casually turning from the window where he and Ivy stood, watching a small fire burn in a field relatively close to the hotel.

"Can I get back in the shower?" I asked.

"Yes," Mike said with a smirk.

"I got really worried when Emilia said there was a fire."

"Don't you think I would come and tell you?" he asked.

"Well, not if you'd already succumbed to smoke inhalation," I reasoned.

"Get back in the shower," he commanded.

"That fire is awfully close to that gas station," I said, peering over his shoulder. I wanted to watch with them, but shampoo in the eyes trumps all voyeuristic tendencies. I got back in the shower.

* * *

Taste of Tasmania

My gosh, I love food. If I wasn't an actor,
I could be a completely different body shape right now.

—Hugh Jackman

The next morning, not having been burned to death, I fired up my laptop and began looking for hotels in Devonport. We had one remaining gap in our itinerary, which was the night before we'd board the ferry to return to Melbourne. The cabin we'd stayed in for one night when we arrived in Tasmania was completely booked, but Devonport is Tasmania's main port of entry, and I was sure we could find something else.

I tried a hotel above an Irish pub, with fleeting visions of a pint of Guinness, but it was booked. Another hotel was booked. A motel was booked, but the clerk assured me that her place of work wasn't suitable for children anyway.

"I wouldn't bring my own children here," she whispered into the phone.

"Oh, wow. Thanks for the heads-up."

Eventually we found a suite at a fairly cheap motor lodge. While I'd been searching for accommodations, Mike was scrolling through events in the area and found out about the Falls.

"It looks like there's this concert series happening," he said. "It's three days, and you camp there."

"That sounds awful," I said.

"But sort of cool?" he asked.

"No, just kind of awful." I don't think camping is awful, and I don't think music festivals are awful, but we didn't have gear. We had kids and an amount of luggage that I believe could be aptly described as a "shit ton."

"Besides," I added. "We don't have tents or anything."

"But you can actually rent gear there," he said.

"Do you even like music festivals?" I countered.

"Okay, never mind."

It's not that we don't like music, but there's something about the idea of loud music and a big crowd that makes me panicky, and Mike shares this reaction. There's also the pressure at such events of not knowing exactly what to do. Should I dance, stand, sway, or sit? Should I clap and nod my head? Sing along? No matter which course of action I choose, it will be entirely forced, which only highlights my dorkish tendencies and the fact that I'm not fully invested in the experience. When you tell people who love concerts that you're just not that into them, they look at you as if you abuse animals or get your daily high from a bottle of spray paint. It's the what's-wrong-with-you look that they are incapable of masking, and every interaction with them thereafter is tainted by their knowledge that when it comes to your existence as a human on this planet, you're plainly deficient. But after a while of being viewed in such light, you get used to it.

With the motor lodge booked, we readied ourselves to

return to Hobart, where we'd visited the Salamanca market, this time to check out the Taste of Tasmania. This is Tasmania's largest food and wine festival, and it takes place every year for a few days over the New Year.

It rained on the drive to Hobart, enough to slow traffic. The pace was nice because at least driving slower saved us from the annoying beep of the car, admonishing us every time we went over 100 kilometers per hour. But as the rain continued, it necessitated using the windshield wipers, the sound of which turned out to be even more annoying than the reprimanding beep.

"This car is a piece of crap," Mike noted.

"Yes," I patted the dash, "but it serves its purpose."

We crossed Break-Me-Neck Hill and Bust-Me-Gall Hill, and we drove past thousands of sheep and Tasmania's teeny tiny police stations, no bigger than Triabunna's Fish Van but just as endearing.

At the festival, we found event parking and exited the car to a lingering drizzle.

"Where are the jackets?" Mike asked.

"The girls have their jackets on," I said.

"Yes, I know that. But where are *our* jackets?"

This was Mike giving voice to yet another of my deficiencies. I tidy without relent. When we'd returned from Freycinet, I'd taken our jackets inside, because I am emotionally wounded by the idea of unnecessary items being left in a vehicle. I think this stems from a now-deceased relative whose car was the vehicular equivalent of a hoarder's house. This doesn't just mean I keep a clean car, but also that I remove items from a car when they really should be in the car. Which is what I'd done with Mike's jacket and my own.

"Um, I think they're back in the closet, hanging up," I mumbled, then physically beat down the shiver that threatened to shake my body in response to the cold. I also pretended that the raindrops hitting my glasses weren't clouding my vision.

We paid a parking attendant, who then smiled and said something to me. I could not decipher a single word of the entire sentence he spoke. I nodded and smiled, and we quickly walked away.

"What did that guy say?" Mike asked.

"I have absolutely no idea."

The main hall of the Taste of Tasmania bustled with food and wine vendors; long tables lined the middle of the hall where people crammed in. It was as loud and crowded as any music festival, but when the focus is on food and wine, the surrounding conditions are always tolerable. Mike ate a Greek wrap of some sort while I indulged in chili mussels. I've always been a fan of mussels, and if you add some spice to them, you're speaking my language (unlike the parking attendant). We purchased a giant hot dog for the girls, which was their equivalent of gourmet excitement.

We met a nice young couple and asked them if it was worth it to come back on New Year's Eve for the fireworks.

"Well, it's a lot like this," the man said, motioning around. "But a lot more people and a lot of people who are really pissed." It took me a moment to make the cultural translation; pissed means drunk, as opposed to angry.

"I wouldn't bring kids here," the woman agreed, and I appreciated the honesty.

"What do you think about the Falls?" Mike asked.

"Can we do the teacups now?" Emilia interrupted.

"Yes," I said, because I didn't want Mike to actually think that we were going to camp for days at a remote Tasmanian music festival with two children under the age of ten. Of course we could have. I just didn't want to.

We said farewell to the young couple and made our way to the children's area.

"Teacups? You guys are too old for teacups," Mike objected.

"I know you'd rather take our kids to Woodstock, but how about we just let them do the little teacup ride?"

"Fine," he said.

"Yay!" they cheered.

And while Emilia was certainly the tallest of all the children to ride the classic teacup ride, it wasn't inappropriate, and the children had fun. And I thought we should enjoy and prolong the innocence as long as possible.

Hobart buzzed with activity. A short walk from the Taste of Tasmania festival, the piers jutting into Sullivan's Cove were crowded with spectators. The annual and grueling Sydney to Hobart yacht race had come to an end. The competitors looked both exhilarated and exhausted, while fans and curious onlookers milled about. The excitement of the race was tempered, only mildly, by the fact that a Cessna had crashed in nearby Storm Bay, killing a twenty-nine-year-old pilot and sixty-one-year-old photographer who'd been filming the race. I told myself the lack of an appropriately somber mood was due to the fact that many of those in attendance might not yet have heard the tragic news. I would later learn that a total of nine competitor boats abandoned the race to assist in searching the waters where the plane entered, nose first, though only a headrest and headphones would be recovered.

When parents learn of tragedy, the question always hovers of how much to share with your child or whether to shield them from it. I tend to share, while Mike shields, which culminates in making me the more depressing parent. At times, the immediate future comes into play, as I'm reluctant to tell my children about a plane crash a week before asking them to board a plane.

Before we left the Taste of Tasmania, we decided to take one more pass at tasting the food and wine offered. In my thinking, that's the way to enjoy a food and wine festival. You eat immediately upon arrival, then spend time watching the performers, letting your kids go on rides and get their faces painted, until you are hungry again, so that you can eat once more before departing. We separated for a bit, as I sat with the kids in one area while Mike went to purchase berries for us to share, not from Kate's Berry Farm, and hopefully ones that wouldn't equate to extortion.

When he returned with a heap of strawberries and blackberries, crowned with a dollop of cream, he looked shaken, and I had the momentary fear that he'd emptied our bank accounts to afford Tasmania's inexplicably expensive berries.

"Everything okay?" I asked.

"Yes," he said. "But I walked by this table, and there was this abandoned baby."

"Oh my god."

"And it looked like it might actually roll off the table."

"Oh my god!"

"So I went closer to try to save it."

"And?"

"And then I realized that dolls these days are really lifelike. And then the little girl who apparently owned it came back for it and gave me looks like I was molesting her doll."

"Ooh." I cringed. "Well, kudos for trying to do the right thing."

In an effort to save our children from spending New Year's Eve with a crowd of pissed people, we instead returned to our "home" in White Beach. As we drove back, I noted that many Australians are inventive regarding their use of trailers and other living accommodations on the Tasman Peninsula, giving some of the least enticing makeshift homes names like "Camelot" and "The Manor." I wondered how many of these places were rented out to travelers who booked online only to arrive and find that their accommodations involved a double-wide and patchwork sheet metal or comparable peculiarity. I thought of the Great Southern Hotel in Melbourne, the oddity of our current residence, and determined that I numbered among those unsuspecting travelers myself.

* * *

MONA

Visiting MONA is like peering through the looking glass.
Deep down in the museum's cavernous underbelly—inside that
mirrored box building—sits Wim Delvoye's cloaca machine, otherwise
known as "the shit machine." The Belgium artist's vast array of
whirring tubes and bags mimic the workings of the human digestive
system. The apparatus is fed food and produces poo. Isn't modern art,
Delvoye seems to say, just a load of crap?

—Clarissa Sebag-Montefiore, "Australia's Temple of Weird"

My main goal when visiting Hobart's Museum of Old and
New Art, known as MONA, was not to be naked at any
time during my visit. I don't have any history of stripping at
art museums—or any inclination to do so—but a friend in the
States had shared with me an article about MONA's controversial, after-hours naked tours. Apparently you could sign up for
this special tour where attendees met in a big room, undressed,
then toured the art museum in the nude, before gathering at
the museum bar for a drink, and then finally redressing themselves. The only thing I really liked about this idea was that the
museum had a bar, and I decided that all museum experiences
could be enhanced if one had a cocktail in hand.

But as for the naked part, I was unconvinced. What was
the point of being naked? To get closer to the artist's message?
What if the halls between exhibit rooms were very narrow? I'd

spend the whole time in fear of brushing up against a fellow nude. What if I sneezed and experienced the unfortunate but common occurrence of slightly wetting my pants? I would have no pants to wet. I'd just be standing there in a small but undeniable puddle of my own urine, pretending to understand modern art. I thought of museums as being over-air-conditioned and brightly lit. Could I be naked and cold in a roomful of strangers? And would I really pay money for such discomfort?

I'm not sure if they still do the naked tours. Perhaps you have to have a secret code word to find out about it or get a personal invite from the museum's founder, rumored to be an eccentric, part-time recluse and math genius who made millions gambling on the Internet. In any case, I didn't see the naked tour advertised, and even if I had, we had the ultimate excuse for not pursuing such a thing, in that we didn't know of any available babysitters. And while I was pretty sure I didn't want to participate in nude art viewing, I was damn sure my kids wouldn't be anywhere near such an event.

We settled for general admission, and on the morning of our trip to MONA, I put on a little black dress and makeup. Most of our Australian experience had found me in the role of dirty hippie, and I decided that for a swanky and controversial art museum, I would go the extra mile.

While I prettied myself and Mike gave the girls breakfast, minus any creepy sausages, which I refused to set eyes on for our few remaining days in Australia, we again tuned in to Tasman Peninsula radio. We heard the last half of Bette Midler's rendition of "Tell Him" before the deejay came on.

"I just love Bette Midler," he said. "I just love her so much. That was 'Tell Him,' but I just love it so much that we're going to play it again."

Maybe he sensed that listeners like ourselves had tuned in halfway through the previous song, and he wanted to make sure we had a chance to hear it in its entirety. When he returned, we heard a second voice in the studio, this one female.

"How did you ring in the New Year?" he asked her.

"I went to bed about half past ten," she said. And I couldn't help but think that she was my kind of woman.

"Are you ready for more Bette Midler?" he asked.

"Definitely!"

"Okay," he said. "I'm going to press the button now."

We turned the radio off, ready for a respite from Bette. I wouldn't consider myself a Midler fanatic, though I also hold nothing against her. Like all good American teenage girls in the eighties, I bawled with abandon while watching *Beaches* with my best friend. But on that morning in southern Tasmania, it was apparent that the deejay had every intention of playing the entire Bette Midler *It's the Girls!* album, and "Tell Him" was only track five out of fifteen; it just seemed a little much. If I was sensitive to too many back-to-back Midler tunes, I wondered how I'd react to more than sixty thousand square feet of galleries displaying modern art. My hopes were high.

MONA sits atop a hill, and the drive to it is flanked on either side by vineyards. Mike dropped us off and then parked the car, as doing so required him to drive a quarter mile away. The place was packed. Two large pyramids sat out on the front lawn. You could enter one of them and experience dim lighting and a gentle voice speaking to you, a sensory experience. In the other were dozens of large beanbags, so that pyramid attracted children who piled in and wrestled as if it were a giant ball pit. I was relieved to see that we weren't the only people who had brought their kids. This indicated that aside from the after-hours naked tour, MONA would be appropriate for all ages. It was a beautiful day, and while the kids played in the beanbags, I surveyed the grounds. There was an open-air bar that just beckoned me to order a glass of wine, though I refrained since it was not yet noon. Instead, I kept one eye on the kids while taking in the large lawn with a stage at one end and a restaurant. A bar will always be first to attract my attention, but a restaurant comes in at a close second. I waited for some time before I saw Mike trudging up the hill.

"Well, this looks cool," he said, then immediately went to the bar and ordered himself a beer, which was the nudge I needed to order myself a glass of wine.

After our drinks, we retrieved the girls from the pyramid of beanbags and walked down a wide set of stairs to the museum's entrance. It was crowded and borderline claustrophobic as we purchased our tickets, but soon after, we moved into a large, open room filled with individual glass cases. The first one I walked up to held a book by an Idaho author I know. What were the chances of such a thing? Is the idea of an Idaho author considered exotic? Other objects in the case dealt with Idaho and for some reason gave me the impression that it was a homage of sorts to Hemingway's suicide.

Emilia and Ivy darted from case to case and peppered me with questions about what was in them, none of which I could explain very well.

"Well, that's a book. And that's a picture of a man. And that's . . ." I stopped as I realized that I was staring at a picture, an action shot really, of a large penis ejaculating onto a piece of lettuce. "Let's go over here," I said and herded them away. Art is, of course, subjective.

"Excuse me, please don't touch," a man said. And I realized then that each case had a guard of sorts standing nearby to keep people from placing their hands on the glass cases. But isn't that what glass is for? To protect the objects underneath?

We moved into another room, and I marveled at the architecture of the building, which to me was the most impressive of all the exhibits. We saw the cloaca machine, a working representation of the human digestive system, which reeked as much as I guess the insides of all of our intestines do. We saw a Fat Car by Erwin Wurm, whimsical and perhaps my favorite of the art, an obese vehicle with grossly exaggerated and bulbous curves, which I took as a commentary on the ridiculous excesses of modern society and its absurd markers of wealth.

Borderline was a display of television monitors, each of which showed a headshot of a person singing Madonna's "Borderline," which oddly made me long for the Bette Midler marathon. Another room housed a replica of what appeared to be a tortured and sexualized tween girl, which made me uncomfortable, but maybe that was the point. I certainly hope the intention was to inspire feelings of discomfort, and I couldn't help looking around the room and wondering which patrons saw it and instead felt feelings of arousal.

"Let's move to a different area," I said to Mike, but the building takes you where it wants you to go, intentionally funneling you into tighter spaces and further claustrophobia. While earlier I'd thought the building was beautiful and my favorite part of the experience, I now began to feel anger toward it. We continued on, and I realized that we were walking by a wall that displayed more than a hundred sculptures of lady parts, each one different, painfully detailed, and hanging on the wall at eye level. Don't get me wrong—vaginas are wonderful. I happen to have one of my own, and it's a downright glorious thing. But I sped past that wall with my kids, directing their attention to anything else I could find. I wasn't prepared for an anatomy lesson.

I decided then that modern art, for me, often feels like a music concert. I'm not quite sure what to do with myself. I looked to the crowds of attendees surrounding me, people who'd paid a fair amount of money for admission into this overly sexual and macabre museum, and noted that most of them stood in front of the artwork but stared at screens in their hands. Most of the screens were small informational devices provided by the museum. Instead of reading about an exhibit on a placard, you could retrieve information on your person-alized mini computer. Others checked e-mail on phones. And that was the most telling, ironic of all of these experiences, the fact that these people were surrounded by art, in turns jarring and disturbing and fantastical, and still their attention was directed instead to a screen of some sort. Maybe no one there knew exactly what to do with themselves.

"I have to get out of this place," I said to Mike.

"Yes," he agreed. "Let's be done with this."

We exited the building, and I took a breath of open air, shedding my panic at the confined spaces of a moment before. I wanted to go back to the open lawn where the kids could play on beanbags and I could drink wine and no one would have to look at replicas of genitalia or action shots of ejacu-lation or see and smell the workings of the human digestive system. But the sun was now out in full force, the lawn was crowded with little shade, and the restaurant was completely packed.

"Maybe we should just go," Mike said.

We agreed to walk together to the car and then drive and try to find another restaurant to grab some lunch. As we left the museum, we passed by a parking spot reserved for God, and next to it was one for God's Mistress. I assumed these were for the museum's founder and his . . . mistress. Whether it was meant to be funny or sacrilegious or just an expression of arrogance, I'm not sure, but I think it achieved, in some measure, all three.

The walk to the car included sweating and whining. We got in, turned the air-conditioning on, and I gave the kids each a small candy cane to keep the peace.

"Well," said Mike. "What do you want to do?"

"Whatever you want to do is fine," I said.

"No, don't do that. Let's actually make this a group decision."

"Okay."

"We could find a restaurant, we could go back home, we could go back to the Taste of Tasmania festival. That's still going on." This was one of those instances in which your spouse attempts to present three different options, but you know which one he's hoping for. Mike wanted to return to the Taste of Tasmania, but I was exhausted and wanted to be done with crowds and parking issues.

"I don't really want to go back to the festival," I said and saw his shoulders slump. "Let's just go find a restaurant somewhere."

We drove around in an area of Tasmania in which restaurants are apparently prohibited. But then I saw a sign indicating the route to the Cadbury Factory. As in the oddly-appealing-to-me-as-a-child eggs that now kind of gross me out. "Let's go to the Cadbury Factory." I could tell he wasn't thrilled with the idea but was half-willing to give it a try, and I felt that I still needed something like the Cadbury experience to make up for the Australian Nougat Company—as well as to wash away the recent overdose of "art."

Mike followed the sign, and then at a stoplight, he inexplicably turned in the other direction. I bit my tongue. A minute later, he said, "Well, what do you want to do?"

"Don't ask me what I want to do," I snapped. "I told you what I wanted to do. I wanted to take the kids to the Cadbury Factory."

"I don't know where it is," he said. "It's not here."

"Yes, it is. You just turned for no reason."

"No, I didn't."

"Go that way," I demanded, and directed him back on the route the signs had indicated. We reached the stoplight from before. "Now go straight. You turned early, for no apparent reason."

Mike huffed, and I clenched my teeth. After another minute, we pulled into the parking lot of the Cadbury Factory. It was incredibly sparse when compared with MONA.

"This is going to be fun!" I said with forced determination and joviality. "We'll have lunch in the café and take the tour. It'll be great."

As soon as we got out of the car, another couple with a toddler spoke up. "Are you here for the tour?" they asked.

"Yes," I nodded.

"It's closed for the holidays," they informed me.

And this is why, when Mike asks what we should do, I say whatever you want to do is fine, because my ideas tend not to work out. We got back in the car.

"What do you want to do?" Mike asked.

And foolish me, I wasn't yet ready to give up on possibly having a good idea. "Let's go to the Sorrell Farm," I said. This was supposed to be a berry-picking opportunity. A real one, not like Kate's overpriced Berry Farm where you could pay ten dollars for a scoop of lavender ice cream with a raspberry on top.

"Okay," Mike said, and I could again tell that it pained him to do so and that he still felt that we should just go back to the Taste of Tasmania in Hobart.

We got on the highway to head to Sorrell and within two minutes found ourselves in the middle of traffic standing still. There was no escape, no inching forward. It was stagnant for so long that people began turning off their engines.

"This is bad," I said.

"Yep," Mike agreed.

"I can't win."

"Nope."

"And you know it's only a matter of time before someone has to poop."

"Mom," Ivy said from the backseat, and I dreaded what she might say. "I'm hungry."

"Just eat your candy cane, sweetie," I said.

"I did. I'm still hungry."

"Me too," Emilia added.

"Okay, let's see." I took stock and found that we were in possession of water and one overripe banana. I peeled it and handed them each a half, waiting to hear complaints.

"Ooh, yay, banana!" Ivy said.

"Yum," Emilia agreed.

When traffic mercifully resumed movement, we drove to the Sorrell Fruit Farm, and I knew as soon as we parked that this was the berry-picking experience I'd been hoping for. Before going to the orchard, we headed to the restaurant for lunch. We sat down outside and ordered from a young waitress. I was sure this would salvage the day, until she returned a minute later and informed us that the kitchen was no longer serving the lunch menu but that they did have a few items still available from the café menu. All was not lost, but again I felt I couldn't win. After sharing waffles topped with ice cream and berries, we went to the actual berry picking. Each with our own container, we entered a large orchard. It was berry-picking nirvana, with strawberry fields, cherry trees, and berry bushes aplenty, tayberries, silvanberries, jostaberries, and others I'd never heard of before, but all resembled a variation of raspberries or blackberries. And in the hot sun, with melting makeup and my little black dress, we filled our containers with berries and managed to have an enjoyable time.

* * *

Dead on the Water

Punctuality is the virtue of the bored.

– Evelyn Waugh

When it was time to leave the White Beach home for the last time, I undertook the sizable task of making a final decision on which seashells would be kept and which would be left behind. This sounds like a waste of time, the silly actions of a child, but I'd come to love the shells fiercely. During our travels, I'd repeatedly tell myself that I wouldn't collect any more, but then we'd travel south, and the closer we moved to the Tasman Peninsula, from when we started in Queensland months before, the more intricate and impressive the shells became.

Emilia and Ivy helped me lay all of the shells out on the tiny concrete landing outside of the front door. We washed each shell in a bucket of water and then returned it to dry in the sun. When dry, each shell had to undergo the final sniff test: if it smelled of rotting remnants of the sea, it would be left behind. The problem was most of the shells passed the sniff test, and I ended up with close to a hundred shells with which I could not bear to part. There were whelks and conchs and cones, iridescent abalone shells, shells of gastropods and bivalves. In short, I'd somehow fallen in love with mollusk remains.

"I guess it would be silly for us to take all of these back to the United States," I said.

"It is a lot of shells," Emilia agreed. They lay in a calcium mosaic before us, the largest the size of a cantaloupe, down to minuscule delicates no bigger than a sesame seed.

"What if you two gave a shell to each of your classmates back home?"

"And one for my teacher," added Ivy.

"And definitely one for Mrs. Barry," Emilia said, determined to make sure her beloved school librarian wasn't left out.

Taking shells back as souvenirs allowed me to justify their continued occupation of precious real estate within our luggage.

"Okay, this one's for my teacher," Ivy said.

"Wait," I protested. "I really love that one."

"Mom," she reasoned, "this is only going to work if you let go."

"You're not supposed to be this insightful at the age of five."

"What's insightful mean?"

"I'm just telling you that you're very smart," I said.

"I know."

When we left White Beach for the return drive to Devonport, we decided to stop in Richmond, a popular and historic Tasmanian town. We walked around and checked out the Richmond Bridge, famed as being the oldest bridge in Tasmania and also built using convict labor. A stream runs below the Richmond Bridge, and it is an ideal and picturesque setting, apparently often used as a site for weddings. A small wooden platform or makeshift mini dock allowed people to peer safely into the stream, and children could feed ducks from there. Some children shared their bread with Emilia and Ivy, and when I observed closer, I saw that they were feeding not only ducks but also eels swirling in the water, jockeying for position. I'd never seen eels outside of an aquarium before and would never have guessed that I'd first do so in Tasmania, or that they'd be happily gobbling crumbs of bread thrown to them by children.

"Should we get something to eat?" I asked Mike. A busy café sold croissants, cappuccino, and a variety of small pies. By that time, I'd come to think of Australia as the land of little pies, and I indulged in a curried scallop, while Mike opted for the more traditional meat pie.

We continued north, eventually passing the ominously named Female Factory in Ross, one of many in Australia, which at first appeared to be the ladies' equivalent of the Port Arthur prison. The word "factory" is used because the women convicts produced wool or another material. If they survived their factory sentence, they were doled out as servants to respectable people or as wives to their male ex-convict counterparts. The conditions at the Female Factory were, sadly, what you might expect of a prison in the 1800s, and then some. The mortality rate for both the female convicts and their babies was high enough to draw public criticism during its time of operation.

Driving through small Campbell Town, it was picturesque and intriguing enough that Mike slowed the car to a crawl in the middle of town. He was startled by the sound of a horn from behind him.

"Jeez, people," he said.

"Well, if you're going to stop driving, maybe you should pull over," I suggested.

"I was just taking a look at things," he said. "What's the big deal?"

"I don't know, honey. People tend not to like it when you suddenly stop driving in the middle of the road." I'm sure, by comparison, Mike sees my driving as hasty and aggressive. While I view intersections as areas to be traveled through as fast as possible, to get out of danger, Mike traverses them as slowly as possible. In his mind, if there is an impact, the damage will be minimal because of his slower speed, while I see his slower speed as increasing his chances of an impact.

We had a fair drive ahead of us, and in an effort to not be a backseat driver the entire trip, I began reading aloud to Mike. The girls were asleep in the back, and I had a copy of Mary Shelley's *Frankenstein* handy, which I wanted to read so that when we returned to the United States, I might return to my book club without a hitch. There was something oddly fitting about reading *Frankenstein* while driving through the Tasmanian countryside.

We finally reached Devonport and checked into our hotel with half the day still before us. We used the pool, which was indoors and heated. If I have to go into a pool, something I try to avoid for the most part, that is the kind of pool I want it to be.

We decided to venture out and see what else Devonport had to offer. Our previous night in Devonport, when we'd first arrived in Tasmania, had left little time for exploration.

As usual, Mike immediately drove us in the direction of water. We got out and looked out over a rocky area. "Let's get back in the car. We're going there," Mike announced, pointing to an area a mile away where the beach appeared to be heavily populated. There was a playground of some sort and the faint sound of live music.

We drove to the area, parked, and found ourselves in the middle of Sangria Sunday, a weekly Devonport event bringing together good food, live music, and potent sangria. The band was called the Sun Kings and played swing music. Couples danced on the lawns, and I could tell they weren't there to merely shuffle their feet and sway their hips. These were trained swing dancers strutting their stuff. I drank sangria, we ate burgers and fries from the restaurant, and the girls danced together on the lawn. Most of the time when my daughters dance, people are happy to allow them space, but space was at a premium, and I could tell that the adult dancers took this event seriously and didn't want any sort of cute little girl getting in the way or stealing the show, so we herded them to the side a few times.

As Sangria Sunday brought our final day in Tasmania to a close, I was eager to get back to the room and get everyone put to bed.

"We are getting up early," I told Mike.

"I know."

"I am not going through the stress we went through last time getting to the ferry."

"I know."

"We're going to be there when they first start boarding," I insisted.

"I know."

He'd felt the stress of the last time, as well, and this time easily capitulated to my demands to show up excessively early.

And we did. We were bright and early and made it through customs without a hitch, with a good half hour of sitting in a parking lot waiting for the ferry to be ready to load vehicles. We listened to the radio, a fascinating episode of International Book Club, while the girls played with their *Spirit of Tasmania* bags in the back, unconcerned with the fact that these were exact replicas of the bags they'd received on the first trip. And since they now had two sets of everything, I was determined to convince them to share certain items with me. For instance, I wanted my own *Spirit of Tasmania* luggage tag.

"Maybe we should turn this off." I gestured to the radio.

"Why?"

"I don't know. I just don't want to have a dead battery or anything."

"It's fine." He waved a hand in dismissal.

"Okay," I mumbled.

Twenty minutes later, it was finally time to board. Mike turned the key in the ignition, and nothing happened, and it was all I could do to keep from screaming, "Damn it, I *knew* it!"

I wanted to hide under the floor mat. All of the cars waited in neat lines, and now the cars behind us were stuck, penned in, and missing their rightful chance to board. All of the people who, like us, had deliberately shown up early, were now being bypassed by the latecomers because we'd drained our battery.

Instead of hiding under the floor mat, I exited the vehicle with Mike, who inquired to all of the surrounding vehicles if anyone had jumper cables. Meanwhile, I profusely apologized to anyone who made eye contact with me. And later I would see this as a clear instance of when women make ridiculous apologies that they don't really need to make, but which we do because we somehow feel we are a disappointment to the world. When I apologized to one of the ferry terminal employees, he looked at me with curiosity.

"Oh, no worries," he said. "It's a daily occurrence."

And of course it would be.

Jumper cables were located, and our piece-of-shit vehicle was brought to life like Frankenstein's monster and with just as much appeal. We drove aboard the ferry, parked as was directed, then got out of the car to travel up to the passenger decks. We grabbed our backpacks and were about to lock the car.

"Can I take my blankie?" Ivy asked.

"Yes, Ivy, you can take your blankie."

"You know, Ivy," Emilia said, "blankies are kind of for babies. Someday you're going to have to get rid of your blankie." Ivy's lower lip stuck out.

Emilia has never been attached to blankies and stuffed animals the way that Ivy has. In fact, Ivy's blankie is faintly inscribed with a Sharpie-written "Emilia" because it was once hers. But Ivy has been extremely attached to the blankie for the full five years of her life. It doesn't cause tantrums or problems or travel everywhere with her, but we do throw it in the backseat during long car trips, and I found no reason to make her feel bad about her attachment. Apparently Mike agreed with me.

"You know, some people keep their blankies forever," Mike said.

"What?" Emilia asked. "Even when they are an adult?"

"That's right," I confirmed.

"Mommy still has her teddy bear," Mike added.

"You do?" Emilia asked.

"She sure does," Mike answered for me. "She doesn't still sleep with him, but she kept him because he's important to her. His name is Pot Belly Bear." All of which is true, and I wanted nothing more at that moment than to throw my arms around my husband. Because the inclination for many men would be to pretend to have no knowledge of such a thing, or to acknowledge it disparagingly. Yes, my husband knows my teddy bear's name, and he's not afraid to say it.

We located our cabin on the ship, and Emilia and Mike began to doze. Ivy, I could tell, was not at all tired. So she and I took a trip to the ship's gift shop. Mike's birthday was in two days. We would be in Melbourne, and I wanted to have something, no matter how small, to give to him. After much deliberation, we settled on a pen, a mug, and a pack of cashews.

* * *

Melbourne Again

I would feel as if I were drugged, sitting there,
watching those damned dolls, thinking what a success
they would have made of their lives if they had been women.
Satin skin, silk hair, velvet eyes, sawdust heart—all complete.

—Jean Rhys, *Good Morning, Midnight*

Three nights remained of our journey. Then we'd under-take another twenty-four hours of travel to reach home in Boise, Idaho. We'd been pretty scarred from our previous stay in Melbourne at the (not so) Great Southern Hotel, so when we booked this final leg of our trip, we went all out. We booked a suite—or the equivalent of a swanky two-bedroom apartment—at the Pegasus Apart'Hotel on A'Beckett Street, a region of Melbourne that advocates excessive use of apostrophes. It was also less than a block from the Queen Victoria Market, which was apparently something worth seeing.

We settled in, and while Mike caught up on e-mails, I suggested the girls accompany me to check out the hotel pool. We followed the signs, which led us to a hallway blocked off for maintenance. But we could see past the signs that the pool was drained.

"Oh no," I said. "It looks like the pool is closed, girls."

"But there's a little water there," Ivy said, pointing, imagining that we could still have a jolly good time frolicking in an inch or two of water.

"Yes, but I'm pretty sure they're not going to let us use it," I said.

We went to the front desk, and I found out that the pool would unfortunately be closed for the duration of our stay. At that moment, I realized that it would be months before I would again have to put on a bathing suit, and I feigned disappointment for my children's sake but said a silent prayer of thanks.

"Daddy, the pool is closed!" Emilia lamented when we returned to the room.

"Oh, well. That's okay because I just got an e-mail from Peter."

"Peter?" I asked.

"Yeah, the owner of our crappy rental car."

"Oh."

"He can meet us at a train station this evening. So we can drive out to it and take the train back into the city."

Such plans are always easier said than executed. We drove almost an hour to a train station near Peter's suburb, but he'd told us to meet him in the parking lot, and we arrived to find five parking lots. When we eventually located Peter, he'd brought the myriad forms we'd filled out and wanted to painstakingly go through them, line by line. The process took so long that I was worried we might not be able to catch a train back into the city. Peter checked his piece of shit on wheels inch by inch, verifying that there weren't any new blemishes for which we might be accountable.

"We, uh, we have one discrepancy," Peter said meekly.

"What's that?" Mike said, doing little to hide his frustration at how long it was taking to hand over the keys.

"You're over the mileage of the contract," Peter said.

"Yes," said Mike, "and the agreement was that the company would just charge my card for any excess. It's all in the contract."

"Yes, well, perhaps we should call them."

This began a fifteen-minute conversation with the company that brokered these private rentals, the end result being the company's reassurance that they would charge us for the excess, as stated in the contract. When Peter finally appeared like he might release us, he stammered one final question.

"So, did you guys travel around much?" he asked.

"Yeah, you know, just a bit around the area," Mike said.

I quickly suggested to Emilia and Ivy that we play a rousing game of I Spy—before one of them offered details of the extent of our travels.

Finally free, we raced with the girls to the station and approached a kiosk where a clerk smiled at us.

"Hi," I said, out of breath. "There are four of us, and we need to get back to Melbourne."

"Okay, do you have Myki cards?"

"What?" I asked. "I mean, no, we don't have anything."

"Okay, how long will you be here?"

"Not long, we just need this one train ride."

"Oh, that's a shame," she said.

"Why?" I knew there was only one train left that evening, and we needed to be on it. I couldn't imagine what a cab might cost to return us to the swank comfort of the Pegasus Apart'Hotel on A'Beckett.

"Well, because you have to buy the card. And it's a shame if you have to buy the card but then you are actually only going to use it this one time. Do you have any plans to come back?"

AK TURNER

"Uh, maybe," I said, and hurled my credit card at her. "So, two adults and two kids. Are we going to make the train?"

"Sure," she said. "You still have three minutes." She spoke slowly, as if this was all the time in the world, and by the time we raced to the train, Mike and I were drenched in sweat from stress, heat, and the awkward movement of half-carrying, half-dragging our children while constantly reassuring them that everything is just fine.

* * *

The next morning, the girls gleefully presented Mike with his birthday gifts. They presented the pen, mug, and nuts with great ceremony, deciding that for each item, they would both have a hand in the gifting process. This meant that two little girls each held on to one end of the same pen, in order to present it to their father on his birthday. Then they followed suit with the mug and nuts, Mike dutifully responding with wide eyes and enthusiasm each time.

After the ninety-second birthday celebration was complete, we went to the IGA, a mini grocery store a block away, and bought cereal and pasta, cheap and easy foods to sustain us for the rest of the trip. That night, we returned to Vapiano, the fantastic Italian restaurant Mike had found the first time we were in Melbourne, to properly celebrate his birthday with a good meal instead of the Ramen that awaited us in our suite.

Staying in a fancy suite, eating out, and visiting tourist attractions, which we planned to do in Melbourne, largely conflict with our goals as a traveling family of four. None of those things are bad, but doing them frequently compromises what the ideas of vagabonding and a part-time nomadic existence mean to us. It's not about decadence or tourism but about learning about different places and people as they truly are, as opposed to how they portray themselves. As a tourist, you're often likely to see what the destination wants you to see, and we make a conscious effort to occasionally get off that well-worn path, which leads us to odd houses in tiny towns in rural Tasmania or dining on fare from the local Fish Van or hanging in bars where singers hand our child a microphone. These experiences complement fancy suites and restaurants and major attractions, bringing a grounding and more cultural experience to the trip as a whole. Despite that philosophy, there is always the frantic rush at the end of a trip to see what yet might be seen. And I recognized that frenzy creeping over us in Melbourne.

The next morning, we went to check out the famed Queen Victoria Market. I love a good market, and this one truly was the queen of all markets, as well as the largest outdoor market (seventeen acres . . . that's some serious shopping) in the Southern Hemisphere.

"Holy goodness," I said when we entered the food section of the market. "I can't believe we bought all that crap from the IGA."

"No kidding," Mike agreed.

The Queen Vic offered not just souvenirs but every type of food in the world that is better than ramen and peanut butter and jelly. Everything was fresh, homemade, beautiful, cheap, and organic, so much so that I imagined us moving to a Melbourne apartment to live within walking distance of the market. A market that good makes you contemplate such things.

There were seafood vendors, butchers, bakers, cheese makers, a stall dedicated entirely to spices, and one for fresh pastas. Merchants sold wine, pesto, and fruits and vegetables, which was pretty much all I figured I needed to survive, as far as food and drink. And still the market offered anything else you might need, including clothing, pet supplies, hardware, luggage, jewelry, flowers, toys, remedies, and home decor. I found and purchased a handful of woven headbands, because the nomadic nature of our trip had lessened my normally obsessive standards of hygiene and forced me to fully embrace my inner dirty hippie. Mike bought a rope from a hardware stall with the intention of fashioning a carrier for the skateboard on our upcoming journey to America.

I took more than six hundred photos during our trip. Did I take any pictures of the incredible vendors and their wares at the Queen Vic, of the gourmet decadence on display there? I did not. I took one picture during our visits to the market. And I'm ashamed to admit that taking this picture was the equivalent of gawking at a car wreck.

The picture was of Pretty Girl, a terribly inappropriate and topless doll in a box that declared her suitable for ages three and up. She can be yours for only $22AUD, which is about $18 in US currency. But you'd think for that kind of money, she might come with enough fabric to cover up her breasts. And if you are going to include breasts, why omit the nipples? Without the nipples, breasts aren't very useful, unless you use them to catch errant crumbs while eating in the car, or employ your cleavage as a pocket if you find your clothing is without one when you really need one.

It's hard to tell in the picture, but Pretty Girl apparently makes a light and a sound when you press on her belly (or the spot where her belly should be). I didn't do this because, honestly, I was a little frightened of Pretty Girl, or rather frightened of the makers of Pretty Girl and anyone else who might have touched Pretty Girl. But I did wonder what sort of sound she might make. Did she moan with pleasure? Ask to borrow a sweater? Quote Shakespeare? Lament the poverty that reduced her to life in a cardboard box?

Mike and I decided to purchase each of the girls a souvenir from the Queen Vic Market. Needless to say, Pretty Girl didn't make the cut (in truth, I shielded them from even viewing Pretty Girl). Instead, they each picked out a ring. Emilia's was a silver band, which she lost in less than forty-eight hours, while Ivy's was a purple bunny that, against all odds, would make it all the way back to the United States with us.

I wonder about the fate of Pretty Girl. If someone does spend twenty-two Australian dollars purchasing Pretty Girl for a child, I can only hope that child bestows upon Pretty Girl a proportionate set of nipples along with a frock of some kind with which to cover them. Because if Queen Victoria were here, I daresay she would not be amused. There were other children's toys, as well, though they were often unfortunately interspersed with lingerie and something called a "Sex Bell." I guess it can be exhausting constantly telling your partner that you want sex, and if you just lay in bed naked and ring the bell, they can come service you without the need for wasted words.

While three days is, of course, not enough time to see all that a city like Melbourne has to see, it did afford us more opportunity than we'd had in Brisbane or Sydney, where the camper van had necessitated an avoidance of downtown rather than an exploration of it. We visited the massive Melbourne Museum where the children flocked to the Dinosaur Walk, but I was most interested in the exhibit regarding illegal harvesting of organs in the eighteenth century.

The Sea Life Aquarium would have been far more impressive had they not publicized that they have locations all over the world, including eight in the United States. I wanted to believe that we were ending our trip with truly Australian experiences but then reminded myself that learning about sea life was probably better for the kids than a lesson on illegal organ harvesting. Our three days in Melbourne brought stifling temperatures, made trying by our mode of travel, which was primarily on foot and via the free trolley system, though as much as we sweated, I was grateful for the free part, which offset the admission of all the places we visited.

Undeterred by Pretty Girl, we returned to the Queen Vic for a brief tour of the Night Market on our final evening in Australia. It was crowded and pulsing with energy, with fire jugglers and alcohol aplenty. As much as it pained us not to buy a beer or sangria or glass of wine (I was particularly drawn to the Prosecco and Prawns vendor), we couldn't justify spending money on alcohol while we still had plenty of it in our room.

"How drunk do you think we would have to get to consume all of the alcohol left in our room?" Mike asked.

"Too drunk," I answered.

"But leaving it behind feels so wrong," he said.

"I know." That we couldn't take it with us was particularly heartbreaking in light of the fact that Qantas is stingy when it comes to offering passengers drinks.

But after the night market, back in our room, hard choices had to be made. Sure, we had to leave the alcohol behind, but I would not leave behind my beloved seashells, or the fifty-eight tiny bottles of shampoo and conditioner and lotion and body wash that I collected from various accommodations over the previous two months. Mike fashioned a carrying strap to Emilia's skateboard, made from the rope he'd bought at the market. I wedged Ivy's scooter into my suitcase, swaddled in my clothing. I took note of just how much clothing we'd carted around with us. Some of it we'd never even worn, though now we would cart it back to the other side of the world, where it would likely sit in our closets, and we'd neglect to wear it until we took it on our next trip abroad. When it came to the alcohol, we soldiered on and drank what we could.

* * *

Idahome

*A journey is a person in itself; no two are alike. And all plans,
safeguards, policing, and coercion are fruitless. We find that after years
of struggle that we do not take a trip; a trip takes us.*

—John Steinbeck

"Would you like to go on an earlier flight?" asked the Qantas lady, and I soaked in her accent, knowing I'd soon miss it.

The question of going on an earlier flight is always a tricky one, because when it is posed, I'm immediately convinced that one of the two planes in question will go down. If I opt for the earlier flight, am I saving my family from perishing on our originally scheduled flight, or am I moving us from what would have been a safe haven into a large, flying, metal tube of death?

"I guess so," I answered. "As long as we have time."

"You'll have plenty of time," she answered. "And this will give you more time in Brisbane, which is where you'll need it, because that's where you'll have to go through Customs and Border Protection."

Ah yes, my old nemesis. Brisbane Customs and Border Protection.

She finished doing whatever it was she had to do on her computer and then, as she handed me our boarding passes, casually added, "You have twenty minutes."

It occurred to me then that much like the clerk at the Melbourne train station, she and I had very different ideas of what constituted "plenty" of time. Once through security and at the gate, I consider anything less than a full hour an inadequate amount of time. There are many things to consider, like last-minute urination and rearranging the carry-on for accessibility to the most desired items. This time is necessary because what I consider the most desired items will likely have changed from the time I packed the carry-on in the hotel room to my thinking right before we board.

The short flight from Melbourne to Brisbane returned us to Customs and Border Protection, upon which Emilia began singing a song that she'd written two months earlier during our first stay with Customs and Border Protection. She belted it out. The lyrics are simple, as she simply repeats the words *customs and border protection* until she's built them to a suitable crescendo, at which point she finishes with one last "customs and border protection" stretched out for extra flourish and with accompanying jazz hands.

We made it through, and Brisbane Customs and Border Protection officers were no doubt relieved that I was finally exiting their country. When the plane lifted off, I felt a sudden rush of emotion, and my eyes welled. Was it because I'd truly loved Australia? Because this trip was coming to an end? Or were these tears of fear because my options over the next fourteen hours were to crash into the ocean or land in the unique hell that is LAX? Questions like these kept me awake. I couldn't sleep.

At one point during the flight from Brisbane to L.A., I'd watched two mediocre movies, both of which had made me cry, despite their mediocrity, and failed at many things, including a crossword puzzle, Sudoku, and solving the mystery of why I'd been offered only one glass of wine after more than six hours on a plane. I closed the magazine with the games that seemed determined to remind me that I would never be a member of MENSA, gave up on the movies, and decided that my safest bet would just be to put the flight path on the screen in front of me. If you've traveled internationally, then you know that this is the map with whatever section of the world you're traveling in, which alternates with various statistics about your trip. These statistics included, at the moment I opened the flight monitor, the fact that we'd traveled six hours and thirty minutes and had six hours and thirty minutes to go. Remarkable, I thought, that I should have turned the screen on at just such a moment. And I was pleased to see that our flight was a mere thirteen hours as opposed to the fourteen we'd traveled on the way from LAX to Brisbane. The screen changed, offering up more numbers, including that the time at our departure city was 6:30 in the evening, and the time of our arrival would be 6:30 in the morning. By then, I stopped thinking of all of these coincidences as remarkable and instead concluded that we'd been sucked into the Bermuda Triangle of the skies. It was a time warp, or a sick joke, or maybe I had fallen asleep after all. In any case, it made my head hurt, and I was relieved as the minutes ticked by, skewing the numbers from their disturbing synchronization.

I spent the hours wondering about the days ahead. How the girls would assimilate back into their classrooms, whether they'd glide back into their lessons without a hitch or whether my less than stellar execution of homeschooling would be grossly apparent. I wondered what our house would look like and whether or not it would feel like home. To offset some of our expenses, we'd rented it out to three different groups during our absence. Would anything be missing? If it was, would we notice? Would we care?

When the plane landed on US soil, I felt the ironic exhaustion that comes from sitting for hours. I also felt a brief pang of the sadness I'd felt during liftoff from Brisbane. Customs at LAX had become an automated affair, and as I held up my passport to the wrong area of the kiosk, I was reminded of trying to pay with a credit card for the first time at an Australian grocery store. When I finally figured it out, courtesy of Mike's assistance and clear enjoyment that I needed it, a giant picture of my face flashed on the screen. It was horrid, and I physically recoiled. Mike burst out laughing. There I was, glistening with sweat, adorned with an unfortunate rash of acne. The scarf on my head, which I'd thought of as bohemian chic (and of which I'd bought four), now made me look hideous. I knew that if I ever had a mug shot taken, this is what it would look like.

I repeated the process, lifting the children up so that the camera could take their pictures as well, and Mike was last to go, showing off his maddeningly photogenic qualities.

When we made it through Customs and Immigration, it occurred to me that once again, Emilia hadn't peed once during the flight.

"Do you have to go potty?" I asked her.

"Yeah," she answered, "I guess so."

"Okay, we'll go as soon as we get to the gate," I said.

"That's fine. I can hold it."

"We have to run," Mike advised.

And then we began my least favorite sport, running through LAX. I was sure we wouldn't make it and tried to prep myself for the disappointment. When I'm stressed, my body leaks from all ports. I'm a snotty, sweaty mess who may have slightly damp underwear. And it was in this manner that we reached the gate, with just enough time to take my daughters to the glory of an airport bathroom before boarding the plane.

When we did board, the plane was cold, causing my sweat-dampened body to chill faster. Despite the stress and body leakage, and the eagerness to return to a place where I would have the luxuries of both a private bathroom and bed, I couldn't help but wonder where we'd travel to next.

"I just got an e-mail," Mike said, interrupting my thoughts. He was staring intently at his phone.

"Yeah?" I buckled myself and buckled the kids.

"Someone wants to do a home exchange." He smiled, still looking at the phone, apparently pleased with what he was reading.

"Well, it must be someplace warm. Otherwise you wouldn't be excited about it." The plane taxied for takeoff.

"Let's just say," he put the phone down and turned to look at me, "you might want to brush up on your Portuguese."

* * *

Acknowledgments

Thanks are due to Elaine Ambrose, Ruth Knox, Christy Hovey, Michael Kroth, Karen Benning, Betty Rogers, and Rick Just for their sincere feedback, considerable time, and friendship.

Elizabeth Day and Sarah Tregay are two of the most talented (and patient) individuals with whom a writer could hope to work.

Thanks also to the Australian Customs and Border Protection Services for allowing me into their country, Levi and Jennifer Benedict for their unmatched hospitality, and Jennifer and Nathan Tolman, without whom this trip never would have happened.

To everyone we encountered in the Land of Oz, thanks for putting up with me.

Lastly, thank you to my husband and two dynamic daughters for making every day exciting and joyful. Onward!

If you enjoyed this book,
please consider posting a review online.

Follow Vagabonding with Kids at

facebook.com/vagabondingwithkids
twitter.com/VagabondingKids
pinterest.com/VagabondKids/
instagram.com/vagabondingwithkids/

Also by AK Turner

Vagabonding with Kids

TALES OF IMPERFECTION SERIES

This Little Piggy Went to the Liquor Store
Mommy Had a Little Flask
Hair of the Corn Dog

DRINKING WITH DEAD WRITERS SERIES
with Elaine Ambrose

Drinking with Dead Women Writers
Drinking with Dead Drunks

Epigraph Sources

Chapter 1, "Welcome to Quarantine": Australian Customs and Border Protection Service, "ACPBS Poaches Bird Egg Smuggler," *Australian Government Newsroom,* May 21, 2014, accessed online January 23, 2015.

Chapter 2, "Australian Disco": Tourism Australia, "Australia's Animals," *Australia,* accessed online January 23, 2015.

Chapter 3, "Don't Fear the Butcher": David Dale, "Firsts," *Who We Are: A Miscellany of the New Australia* (Crows Nest: Allen & Unwin, 2006), 51.

Chapter 4, "The Crocoseum": *Oxford Dictionaries* (Oxford University Press), accessed online June 2, 2015.

Chapter 5, "Humping the Dingo": Vera Wang.

Chapter 6, "A Formal Apology": Bill Bryson, *In a Sunburned Country* (Broadway Books, 2000), 18.

Chapter 7, "Byron Bay": Albert Einstein.

Chapter 8, "The Sex Lives of Koalas": Koalaexpress.com.au, accessed July 23, 2015.

Chapter 9, "Clean Is the New Black": *Popular Mechanics*, "How to Make Antivenom—and Why the World Is Running Short," Hearst Communications, Inc., May 21, 2014, accessed July 29, 2015, http://www.popularmechanics.com/science/health/g561/how-to-make-antivenom-why-the-world-is-running-out/.

Chapter 10, "Dry Is the New Clean": Jeffrey Archer.

Chapter 11, "Killers in Eden": KillersOfEden.com.

Chapter 12, "Take My Keys": Benjamin Disraeli, *Words of Wisdom*

(Chrysalis, 2004), 210.

Chapter 13, "The Spirit of Tasmania": TheSpiritOfTasmania.com.

Chapter 14, "Can I Get a Witness?": http://www.jw.org/en/publications/books/bible-teach/are-we-living-in-the-last-days/.

Chapter 15, "Port Arthur": http://www.history.com/this-day-in-history/first-australian-penal-colony-established.

Chapter 16, "Have a Solitary Christmas": Emmeline Pankhurst.

Chapter 17, "Children and Other Devils": Natalie Williams, Australian composer.

Chapter 18, "Adventures in Public Toilets": Charles de Lint.

Chapter 19, "Love on the Beach": Wilson Mizner.

Chapter 20, "Burn Out": Ryan Grenoble http://www.huffingtonpost.com/2015/01/09/jeremy-koala-burned-paws-photo-australian-fire_n_6444286.html.

Chapter 21, "Taste of Tasmania": Hugh Jackman.

Chapter 22, "MONA": Clarissa Sebag-Montefiore, "Australia's Temple of Weird," Slate.com, http://www.slate.com/articles/news_and_politics/roads/2015/02/mona_tasmania_s_biggest_tourist_draw_is_a_controversial_museum_featuring.html.

Chapter 23, "Dead on the Water": Evelyn Waugh.

Chapter 24, "Melbourne Again": Jean Rhys, *Good Morning, Midnight* (W. W. Norton & Company, 1999).

Chapter 25, "Idahome": John Steinbeck.